P9-AFR-405

# LONDON

**By the staff of Editions Berlitz**

Copyright © 1977 by Editions Berlitz,
a division of Macmillan S.A.
1, av. des Jordils, 1000 Lausanne 6, Switzerland.

All rights reserved. No part of this book may
be reproduced or transmitted in any form or
by any means, electronic or mechanical,
including photocopying, recording or by any
information storage and retrieval system
without permission in writing from the
publisher.

1985 Edition

Library of Congress Catalog Card Number:
77-73512.

Berlitz Trademark Reg. U.S. Patent Office
and other countries – Marca Registrada.

Printed in Switzerland by Weber S.A., Bienne.

# How to use our guide

- All the practical information, hints and tips that you will need before and during the trip start on page 100, with a complete rundown of contents on page 103.
- For general background, see the sections London and the Londoners, p. 6, and A Brief History, p. 12.
- All the sights to see are listed between pages 20 and 67. Our own choice of sights most highly recommended is pinpointed by the Berlitz traveller symbol.
- Entertainment, nightlife and all other leisure activities are described between pages 68 and 86, while information on restaurants and cuisine is to be found on pages 87 to 95.
- Finally, there is an index at the back of the book, pp. 125–127.

---

*Although we make every effort to ensure the accuracy of all the information in this book, changes occur incessantly. We cannot therefore take responsibility for facts, prices, addresses and circumstances in general that are constantly subject to alteration. Our guides are updated on a regular basis as we reprint, and we are always grateful to readers who let us know of any errors, changes or serious omissions they come across.*

---

Text: Bernard Feller
English adaptation: Ken Bernstein
Photography: Jeremy Grayson
Layout: Doris Haldemann
We wish to thank Sheila Allen, the London Tourist Board and the British Tourist Authority for valuable assistance. The cartography is based upon material from Johnston & Bacon Ltd., Edinburgh.

# Contents

*Cover picture:* Buckingham Palace

# London and the Londoners

You may well fall in love with London—but not at first sight. The world's most habitable great city creeps up on you. No single vista, no instant revelation will bowl you over. Rather, the attractions add up: the sober elegance of a Georgian house, the details of a Victorian pub, a brave show of colour in a windowbox of geraniums. All

at once an accumulation of discreet charms will come into focus and you'll find that just being in this immensely civilized city makes you feel good.

Foreigners often love London, even if the English don't. Provincials feel sincerely sorry for their friends who live in the capital. And most Londoners can hardly wait for the weekend to skip town. But don't misunderstand. They're legitimately proud of their metropolis on the Thames, the one-time capital of empire. They simply prefer the bucolic life.

The mark of social success is to have a house in London—preferably near Sloane Square—and another in the country for long weekends. The Londoner would prefer to banish urban pressures to the middle of the week. This aristocratic style of living is almost everybody's dream. City financiers invest their fortunes in a country life. Prime ministers of all political leanings rush to Chequers for the weekend. And even the Cockney, so deeply attached to the drab East End, dreams of winning

*The stately pace of London: red buses stalled on a bridge; attire is sober around the Law Courts.*

the pools and raising thoroughbreds near Newmarket.

London's population though still above seven million, has been diminishing steadily in a surge to the suburbs near the merciful Green Belt circling the metropolis. Those who remain in the 610-square-mile capital console themselves in their well-tended back gardens, or in the exemplary public parks, which cover 20,000 acres.

Having lost their hearts to the countryside, it's not surprising to find Londoners in communities modelled on village life. They live in Chiswick or Dulwich, Hampstead or Islington, Putney or Wimbledon. Each neighbourhood has its own atmosphere, rhythm and, usually, village square or green. Each of its 32 boroughs runs its own housing, parks and libraries; each levies its own property taxes ("the rates"). Travel from South Kensington to North Kensington and you change en-

*Yesterday and tomorrow : skyscrapers loom above a London cricket pitch.*

vironment completely. The pubs and their customers look different; so do the houses. Even the accents can change within a couple of stops on the underground. The great governmental, financial and cultural centre is not really a city at all, but a juxtaposition of villages.

And it's in these villages, not in the tourist-packed West End, that you'll get the undiluted feeling of London and the Londoners. Every borough's "high street" is a microcosm of this nation of shopkeepers, despite supermarket chains edging out the local greengrocer and butcher, even if decimalization has killed off the half-crown and the shilling and metrication threatens the pint and ounce. In the villages that make up London you'll experience the easy pace and ready courtesy which seem so unusual in a world so tense.

Watch Londoners queueing at a bus stop. Long after normal patience would be exhausted, when commuters in other capitals would be rioting or at least snarling, the Londoners retain their stiff upper lip. And when, at last, an "elephant train" of red double-deck buses does arrive, a dry little joke about the foibles of London Transport will go a long way to ease the pressure.

Where else would eccentrics be coddled so patiently? "Ah, well", the Londoner says, with a tolerant shrug, at the sight of a character advertising the world's impending end or wearing an outrageous costume or laughing convulsively at his own joke. Live and let live is not just a platitude here, it's the practice.

Every Sunday afternoon tolerance reaches its zenith at Speakers' Corner, Hyde Park. Absolutely anyone can climb aboard a soap-box and try to convert the masses. Do you believe the earth is flat? Must immigration be halted? Should the monarchy be abolished? Have a go, but remember that tolerance works both ways; the crowds won't stay to listen unless hecklers are also allowed a say.

All these feverish harangues are delivered under the benign eyes of a couple of London bobbies in their tall helmets, on hand to discourage any outbreak of fisticuffs. Like all uniformed policemen in England they are armed not with guns, but with tact and intelligence—and the support of the people.

The English are reserved, it's true. They don't usually speak to anyone without having been introduced. But British reserve is not just a selfish desire to be left alone, it's based upon a respect for other people's privacy. A Londoner isn't likely to open a conversation, but if a foreigner should break the ice, a friendly dialogue may well ensue. The exception is the **9** underground: it simply isn't done to interrupt a traveller reading a newspaper. One reads one's own paper and avoids looking too brazenly into other faces.

Conversation-starting note: "Excuse me?" is the phrase for getting someone's attention. It means, "May I speak to you?" To beg someone's pardon if you have stepped on a toe or wish to cut through a crowd, don't say "Excuse me", say "Sorry".

As distinctive as London's red pillar boxes and telephone booths, black taxis and umbrella-toting businessmen, is the weather. It has quite a reputation. Every day in London is said to cover all four seasons. You're certainly aware of being on an island. The sea winds sweep the clouds across the sky, changing the mood from rain to sunshine in a flash. Solution: when the first raindrops spatter down, nip into a museum. By the time you come

*Stern as a guardsman, child in busby struts. Right: deckchairs in* *the park face setting summer sun.*

out there's every chance that it will be clear again.

Smog is no longer a problem. London abolished it by banning smoke-producing fuels. Those pea-soup London nights are but a hazy memory. Nevertheless, from habit, Londoners libel their weather, which remains the prime topic of conversation.

Although London is farther north than Medicine Hat or Khabarovsk, the climate is ever mild. Freezing winter nights are rare, and in summer a heat wave is proclaimed any time City gents actually remove their bowlers and jackets. The mean annual temperature is just below 51 degrees Fahrenheit. This is a bit above 10 degrees Celsius, as the Meteorological Office would insist on saying—though no Englishman would admit to understanding such "foreign" measurements. In any language the weather is moderate and kind.

And so are the Londoners.

# A Brief History

Ancient Bretons gave London its name—*Llyn-Din,* Celtic for "lake stronghold". But that gloomy outpost in the marshes of southeast England could hardly have qualified as a town.

It was the Romans who really created London—*Londinium*—in the 1st century A.D. The town came to be one of the most prosperous in the Roman empire, in those times covering roughly the area of the present City of London. Excellent engineers, the Romans built a bridge across the Thames where London Bridge stands today. And 50,000 people settled around two small hills, the present locations of St. Paul's Cathedral and the Stock Exchange. You can still see, affixed to a wall across from Cannon Street underground station, the "London stone" from which point all distances were measured to the far corners of Roman Britain.

### Angles, Saxons and Others
After the Romans beat a retreat in the 5th century, London entered a dark and confused period. To help sort out internal feuds the latinized Celts invited teams of Germanic mercenaries—Angles, Saxons and Jutes. These soldiers of fortune eventually sent the natives packing to Wales, Scotland and Ireland. Finally the warlike Vikings sailed in, creating havoc and terror in repeated raids.

By the beginning of the 9th century, calm and order returned to the troubled country under the rule of the man who's often called the first English monarch, King Egbert. His grandson, Alfred the Great, ordered the city walls of London rebuilt.

In 1066 the Norman armies crossed the Channel and overcame the English defenders at the Battle of Hastings. William the Conqueror, crowned in the newly built Westminster Abbey, ordered the construction of the Tower of London. Thanks to the Normans, a fresh Latin influence seeped into the developing Anglo-Saxon culture. French became the official language and remained supreme in high circles until about the 15th century, having been gradually supplanted by modern English (derived from Germanic and Scandinavian dialects, with French dressing).

### Feudal England
The influence of London grew rapidly while the kings of Eng-

land were diverted by more pressing affairs—warring in France or setting forth to the Crusades. Under Henry I the citizens won the right to choose their own magistrates. The elective office of Lord Mayor of London was created in the 12th century in the reign of Richard the Lionheart. In 1215 his brother, King John, bowed to the troublesome noblemen assembled in a meadow called Runnymede and set his seal to *Magna Carta*. This historical breakthrough in the struggle against absolute power had the incidental effect of conferring special privileges on London.

But for all its importance, the city was never the capital of England. The monarchs preferred to keep their distance from those restless citizens organized in trade and craft guilds and jealous of their liberties. Thus the palace of Westminster, and later the palace of Whitehall, became the centres of power. By this tactical choice the kings set the stage for London's expansion: the great noble families were already building magnificent gardened mansions along the Strand, the road linking the palace with the city, a couple of miles downriver.

Nevertheless, until the 16th century, London scarcely over-

*Tourists roam deck of* Cutty Sark, *clipper from great days of Empire.*

flowed the city limits set in Roman days. Then Henry VIII added some desirable domains when he confiscated church property after breaking relations with Rome. With the redistribution of this land and property and the rising tide of commercial interests, the city began to grow. Henry's historic decision, based rather more on **13** his divorce problems than on weighty theological grounds, gave birth to the new Anglican religion. Protestantism was only one of the revolutionary imports from Europe; general intellectual ferment was also spreading to England, setting the stage for the glories of the age of Shakespeare.

## The Elizabethan Era

Before London could burst its medieval boundaries, the citizens needed a sense of security stronger than fortress walls. The answer for an island nation was sea supremacy, and it was achieved in 1588 with the destruction of the hitherto invincible Spanish Armada. In

its own way, the City of London shared in this victory, having raised the money to arm a score of warships.

The reign of Elizabeth I was a particularly productive era. She put some order into the religious situation muddled by her father, Henry VIII. By her personal initiative the foundations were laid for a colonial empire; in 1597 Parliament first decreed transportation to the colonies for convicted criminals. During Elizabeth's reign the authority of the state was strengthened, her subjects became more affluent, and English literature blossomed with the achievements of Francis Bacon, Ben Jonson, Christopher Marlowe and, above all, William Shakespeare.

## Revolution and Restoration

After the fruitful reign of Elizabeth I, her immediate successors were bound to seem disappointing. The reign of James I is remembered for a rash of conspiracies against the crown. In the classic Gunpowder Plot (1605), Guy Fawkes was arrested in the cellars of Parliament as he was about to blast the dignitaries assembled upstairs, king and all.

Charles I, son of James, resisted the new powers of Parliament and plunged the country into a civil war. His career was cut short by the executioner's axe in 1649. The man behind the coup, the puritanical Oliver Cromwell, seized power and forced the warring factions together. Dissolving Parliament, this energetic statesman proclaimed himself Lord Protector instead of king and pushed forward many of the good works of Elizabeth. Unfortunately his religious fanaticism left a somewhat morose imprint on the national character, so deeply embedded that even the joyous Restoration period under Charles II couldn't quite overcome the gloom.

The next great confrontation between king and Parliament blew up under James II, who was distrusted for being a converted Catholic and a sympathizer of Louis XIV. This time the king didn't lose his head; he was allowed to abdicate and flee the country. The Revolution of 1688–9 installed William III and Mary and gave England a stable, constitutional monarchy at last. The Bill of Rights finally and offi-

*Overshadowed by history, visitors swarm through Tower of London.*

cially abolished absolutism and proclaimed the supremacy of Parliament.

## London expands

From a population of about 185,000 in Elizabethan times, London was to become Europe's first city of a million by the end of the 18th century. It would have grown even bigger had it not been for two calamities in the reign of Charles II. In 1665 the Great Plague wiped out one-third of the population and a year later, fire almost eliminated the City of London. The Puritans attributed the five-day catastrophe to God's punishment—or a Papist plot. The Great Fire is commemorated by a stone column tersely known as The Monument.

London expanded westward in a distinctive way. Builders made deals with aristocratic land-owners to construct stately ensembles surrounding green squares. Thanks to these schemes the architecture of London—especially around squares like St. James's or Berkeley—developed into classics of open spaces and harmony.

From square to square London spread: to Mayfair (now the place for elegant pleasures), to Pimlico (with its antique shops), and to Belgravia (the haughty haunt of diplomats). In 1750 a second bridge was finally built across the Thames. Westminster Bridge pointed to further development of the south bank; meanwhile the port of London was rapidly becoming Europe's commercial centre.

Eighteenth-century London was the dynamic, creative capital of a great world power. It was the exciting age of Captain Cook, Adam Smith and the steam-engine man, James Watt. In the coffee houses of London, men as brilliant as Addison, Swift, Pope, Gibbon and Samuel Johnson were holding forth. Handel was at work composing his *Water Music* to herald the royal barges on the Thames. Kew Gardens and the British Museum opened.

Overseas, things were booming in the burgeoning empire until a tax dispute caused a spot of trouble with the Americans. The misunderstanding snowballed into a full-scale revolutionary war. To the astonishment of George III the colonists won, and in 1783 Britain formally recognized the independence of the U.S.A. Next came the French Revolution, which sent waves of sympathy across the British working class.

*Horse Guards undergo stiff inspection in dress uniform from another age.*

Just as in the age of Elizabeth, Britain greeted the 19th century preoccupied by problems of power, politics and maritime superiority. The challenge came from Napoleon. Admiral Nelson disposed of the French fleet at Trafalgar in 1805, assuring that Britannia ruled the waves. The Iron Duke, Wellington, triumphed at Waterloo in 1815. So much for Napoleon. Great Britain was now respected—or feared —worldwide.

## The Industrial Revolution

The century of Victoria—she reigned, astonishingly, all the way from 1837 to 1901—saw the triumph of the industrial revolution. British entrepreneurs exploited every breakthrough as the boffins devised increasingly ingenious manufacturing techniques. It was an age for conquering new markets and new colonies. Political power was shifting beyond the aristocracy and landowners to the rising middle classes. Lon- **17** don's prosperity lured workers from the countryside, from Ireland, even from the Continent. To house them the slums of the East End went up in a crash programme (they were to come down later, in the Blitz of the Second World War). The West End was also gaining ground with a proliferation of elegant townhouses worthy of the capital of the greatest empire ever known. There was, in fact, no limit now to the boundaries of London; trains and the world's first underground railway system created a new breed of citizen—the commuter.

During the First World War, German dirigibles bombed London. But it was nothing compared to Hitler's firebombs, which turned the night sky red over London and gutted hundreds of thousands of buildings, mostly in the East End, killing 30,000 people. For protection, civilians slept on underground railway platforms.

The indomitable spirit of World War II London was personified by Winston Churchill, in his billowing "siren suit", cigar in hand, exploring the morning-after wreckage, imploring his people to fight on. He directed the war from the bottom sub-basement of an impregnable stone bastion, now an ivy-covered eyesore in the northeast corner of St. James's Park.

Vast postwar reconstruction changed the skyline of London: new office blocks rose in skyscraper style, and towers mushroomed in public-housing projects. Overcrowding, noise, smoke and prices triggered an exodus to the cleaner, roomier suburbs.

The urban population stabilized around seven million, down from earlier figures, in spite of a heavy influx of fortune-seekers from the former colonies. The colourful presence of so many Indians, Pakistanis, Jamaicans and other Commonwealth immigrants has added much spice to London life.

The population statistics fail to mention a most vital figure: London is swelled by 10 million tourists every year. The British economy couldn't do without them. Tourism has become one of the biggest sources of foreign exchange, after manufacturing, chemicals… and whisky!

*Royal pomp always draws crowds. Thames boatsman seeking solitude glides by new apartment towers.*

# What to See

With so much to see and do, London may exhaust you. Whatever your tastes, you can do everything and find everything in London. It's just a question of knowing where! (For a starter, zip through the yellow pages for clubs, associations and societies dedicated to your hobbies—from archaeology and art to Zen and zoology.)

London's monuments and historical treasures—from relics of the Romans to memories of the Blitz—could fill your whole holiday. And you wouldn't want to miss Buckingham Palace, or the residence of prime ministers, 10, Downing Street, despite its unassuming appearance. You must take in the traditional spectacles such as the Changing of the Guard. And you couldn't leave London without listening in on the unique free-for-all of Speakers' Corner at the Marble Arch end of Hyde Park.

But will there be time? You must explore the antique shops, museums and markets. There's the theatre, opera, ballet, concerts—and who could pass over the shopping with so many top-quality bargains?

## Getting your Bearings

Even if you plan to limit yourself to the best-known tourist attractions, London will be a bit confusing at the outset. The best way to get your bearings is to take an orientation tour. Here are some suggestions:

**Organized tours:** London Transport runs the "Round London Sightseeing Tour", normally in double-decker buses, encompassing all the major sights in two hours. The tour is unguided, but a souvenir route map highlights the main places of interest. Tours leave Piccadilly Circus, Victoria (Grosvenor Gardens) and Marble Arch daily, except on Christmas Day, with at least one departure an hour from each point. London Transport also operates a full programme of guided tours, for example the popular "London Day Tour". For further details, enquire at one of London Transport's information centres at major stations, or call their 24-hour information number (01) 222-1234.

**By boat:** The River Thames has long been the main route between Westminster and the City. In about 20 minutes you can see much of London during the trip between Westminster Bridge and Tower Bridge. It's hard to beat the view of the

Houses of Parliament from the Thames. Boats leave Westminster Bridge, Charing Cross pier or the Tower of London every day, but service is less frequent from October to March. A relaxing way of taking in the panorama as it glides by, is by joining the special lunch and dinner cruises. Details from the London Tourist Board, see p. 121).

**Excursions on foot:** Off-the-beaten-track tours are organized by Off-Beat Tours of London, 66, St. Michael's Street, W.2., and by London Walks, 139, Conway Road, N.14. Conducted by well-informed, experienced guides, there are 40 different itineraries.

### Vantage Points

Another way to get your bearings is an aerial view from the top of a monument or tall building.

● The Hilton Hotel in Park Lane has a roof bar more than 300 feet above Buckingham Palace. The drinks are rather more expensive than at the corner pub, but the view is worth it.

● In the City, there's a magnificent view of the Thames and the port of London from the dome of St. Paul's Cathedral. Unfortunately, you have to climb 727 steps to the top.

● Also in the City, but less than half as difficult to climb, the Monument has only 311 steps.

● For hours of admittance to St. Paul's Cathedral and The Monument, see under HOURS, page 113.

### How to Travel

The **underground** (London's subway system) is as a general rule quick, and for longer journeys especially, the most practical method of travel. But try to avoid the rush hours (8.30 to 9.30 a.m. and 4.30 to 6.30 p.m.).

The advantage of **buses** is that you see London while you're travelling. But you have to master a complicated system of routes—along with the very British art of queueing. Furthermore with the density of London traffic and the long routes buses run, the wait for the next bus can be way above what is indicated at the stop.

The "London Explorer Pass" for unlimited travel on both buses and underground is economical and practical. See pp. 103 und 122 for details.

**Taxis** are not expensive. They're comfortable and reasonably fast except during the rush hours. Taxis are ideal when you have to get to a complicated address.

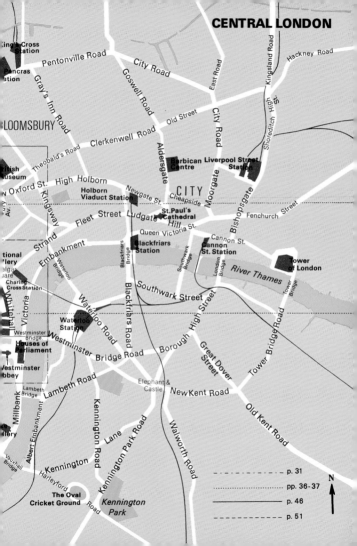

# Westminster and Whitehall

The corridors of power sprawl through Westminster and Whitehall. Symbolic authority centres on Buckingham Palace, the Queen's London home. At Westminster Abbey, nearby, very nearly all of Britain's sovereigns were crowned. Across the street, in the Houses of Parliament, the laws of the land are debated far into the night. Behind the austere façade of Whitehall thousands of civil servants take tea and implement those laws. All this is concentrated in a triangle of London so small you could cover it in less than an hour. When the Queen rides from the palace to parliament or the abbey, the royal coach makes a detour via the Mall and Whitehall. The direct route is simply too short; her subjects and the tourists wouldn't have enough chance to see the monarch go by.

## The Mall and the Palace

The place to start is **Trafalgar Square,** a vast gathering place for tourists and pigeons. It's named after the 1805 Battle of Trafalgar in which Lord Nelson defeated Napoleon's fleet off the Spanish coast. Nelson's statue tops the very tall Corinthian column in the centre of the square. When the square isn't just normally busy, its size and central situation make it ideal for political demonstrations. On the north side is the National Gallery (see p. 63). To the east is the fine 18th-century baroque Church of St. Martin-in-the-Fields. Canada House and South Africa House also face onto Trafalgar Square.

To the southwest from **Admiralty Arch** there is a magnificent view of the **Mall** (pronounced to rhyme with *pal*). The arch was built in honour of Queen Victoria. On the left side of the Mall, **St. James's Park** is majestic and charming. In good weather you can see Whitehall secretaries, and often their bosses, munching sandwiches on park benches. On the opposite side of the avenue is a series of elegant houses: Nash's Carlton House Terrace, Marlborough House, where the Commonwealth is administered, Clarence House, home of Queen Elizabeth the Queen Mother, and Lancaster House. At the far end of the Mall stands Buckingham Palace.

Have a closer look at **St. James's Palace,** a maze of courtyards and passages, reconstructed many times. From 1698 to 1837 this was a royal residence; Queen Victoria preferred Buckingham Palace, but even today foreign ambassadors are officially accredited to the Court of St. James'.

**Buckingham Palace,** behind high iron railings, is interesting not for its architectural beauty but for its role as home of the monarch. The sight of its well-drilled Guards enlivens the

*Banners high: "lollipop lady" halts traffic at school. Trafalgar Square protests happen on most Sundays.*

## Changing of the Guard

Of course there are plenty of official ceremonies. But you may not happen to be in town for the Opening of Parliament, the visit of a Head of State, a royal wedding or coronation. The ceremonial gap is filled by the Changing of the Guard. It's a daily affair in three different places.

● At Buckingham Palace, in front of the main entrance, daily at 11.30 a.m. (alternate days in winter). A 30-minute show with a military band, everyone decked out in busbies and red tunics. Stand in front of the palace or along the route. But be sure to take up your position at least half an hour in advance, especially if you're accompanied by children. The crowds can be dense.

● In Whitehall, the changing of the Horse Guards, with their black horses and golden helmets, is a daily event. 11 a.m. weekdays and 10 a.m. on Sunday.

● At Windsor Castle, daily at 10.30 a.m., with military bands.

picture. The Royal Standard is raised only when the Queen is in residence. Constructed in 1703 for the Duke of Buckingham, the palace was remodelled by Nash in 1825.

In summer the Queen gives royal garden parties on the back lawn. Hundreds of guests, invited in reward for civic achievements glorious or humble, mill about sipping tea and hoping she strolls over for a chat. Nervously searching the sky for rain-clouds, the party-goers discover that there is a fine view of the top of the Hilton Hotel from the palace gardens. And, of course, vice-versa.

*Buckingham Palace by night: flag indicates Her Majesty is at home.*

You can visit the **Queen's Gallery,** where some of the masterpieces of the royal art collection are on view, and the Royal Mews with a display of sumptuous coaches and ceremonial carriages. The entrance is around the left of the palace.

On great royal occasions the deep British feeling towards the monarch—a sentiment shared, indeed, by much of the world—comes to the surface. During coronations, royal marriages and other stately events, such as Elizabeth II's Silver Jubilee, the British can identify with the Queen and her family, who become members of everyone's family.

## The Palace of Westminster

The Houses of Parliament, officially known as the Palace of Westminster, can be seen from afar thanks to the familiar shape of the clock tower. This famous belfry, 320 feet high, contains **Big Ben,** a 13½-ton bell which strikes the hours with a chime known round the world. Note that it's the bell, not the remarkably accurate clock, which is called Big Ben.

The view of the Houses of Parliament is most imposing from a boat in the Thames or from the opposite bank of the river. You may be disappointed to learn that this fine Tudor building with neo-Gothic pin-

nacles and gilded rooftops is a mid-19th-century structure; by British standards that's virtually modern. Most of the ancient palace was destroyed by fire in 1834. In 1941, during the Blitz, the House of Commons was bombed out. It was rebuilt in 1950.

One of the ancient elements still in existence is **Westminster Hall,** at present closed to the public for security reasons.

This huge oak-beamed hall (more than 200 feet long and 90 feet high) was built by a son of William the Conqueror, but in its present state it dates from the beginning of the 15th century. In this hall, the abdication of Edward II was proclaimed, the trial of Charles I took place, and Cromwell was named Lord Protector of the Realm. (Later his head was exhibited here.) In the same hall Guy Fawkes heard his death sentence pronounced for the gunpowder plot.

A flight of steps descends to St. Stephen's Crypt, dating from the 14th century. Unfortunately, its present decoration comes from the Victorian period, the same fate as overtook St. Stephen's Hall.

During parliamentary sessions, the members of the **House of Commons** sit from

Monday to Friday, late into the evening (though winding up early on Fridays for the weekend getaway). Among the more dramatic events, the Prime Minister answers members' questions on Tuesday and Thursday afternoons. And it's at 10 p.m. on any day that parliament is in session that history may be made, for it's at this hour that the voting on crucial bills, including motions of confidence which could topple a government, is held. In an era of computers the Commons continues to vote in its time-tested, simple way, not by voice or ballot or push-button but by bodies. M.P.'s voting "aye" leave the chamber by one door, the "nays" by another. Members of the House working as tellers keep a record of the numbers.

While visiting the Public Galleries is possible, it needs careful pre-arrangement. Not only is the number of entrants restricted, but security precautions are severe. Check first with the London Tourist Board (see pp. 121–122) who will tell you the prevailing situation.

*Neo-Gothic spires of Parliament dominate north bank of Thames.*

From the Commons a passage leads to the **House of Lords,** with members' seats arranged around the throne. This hall is the work of the 19th-century architect Pugin, apostle of the neo-Gothic. The Royal Gallery is reserved for the sovereign when she visits the Lords; she hasn't the right to enter the Commons!

The **Jewel Tower,** now a museum, is almost all that remains of the medieval fortress of Westminster.

## Westminster Abbey

Much more than just a church, Westminster Abbey, only a few steps from the Houses of Parliament, is a place where the sacred and profane, religion and history, are inextricably mixed. From the 14th to the 16th century, the House of Commons met in the abbey and not the Palace of Westminster.

The abbey still contains a school, which explains the presence of so many school-

### The Oldest Parliament

England had a parliament long before the country became a parliamentary democracy. As early as the 13th century, representatives of the whole country came together for consultations, either in the Royal Palace of Westminster or in the Abbey opposite.

In 1529, Henry VIII abandoned Westminster for Whitehall. Parliament, which by then had split into Commons and Lords, moved into Westminster. Some decades later Parliament affirmed its power by defying the king, eventually leading to the execution of Charles I. William III and Mary signed a Bill of Rights which created a constitutional monarchy, establishing the supremacy of Parliament.

Today there are 635 Mem-

bers of Parliament elected to the Commons by universal suffrage. The leader of the political party obtaining most of the seats in the general election becomes Prime Minister and head of the government.

The House of Lords reviews and sometimes revises Acts of Parliament sent up from the Commons. The chamber consists of about 800 peers, both hereditary aristocrats and others proposed by the Prime Minister and named for life by the sovereign. Under certain circumstances, the Lords have a veto power over legislation from the Commons. Although there are occasional demands for abolition of the Lords, these are usually rejected by the tradition-loving public.

children. (You may even glimpse a soccer game through some half-opened doorway!)

Above all the abbey has been, and still is, a most significant spiritual sanctuary. Until the Reformation, many pilgrims came here to meditate and confess their sins at the tomb of the royal saint, Edward the Confessor. Elizabeth I gave the abbey its present organization—a collegial church under the authority of a Dean who is directly responsible to the Crown. Thus the abbey may be considered the sovereign's church. Here kings are crowned (on an ancient oak throne that contains the historic Stone of Destiny), and royal marriages and funerals take place. The tombs of kings, soldiers, explorers, poets and scholars are here, making the abbey a national shrine.

Westminster Abbey was built in stages. The foundations were laid by Edward the Con-

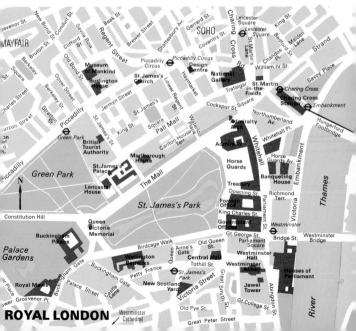

**ROYAL LONDON**

fessor in the 11th century on the site of a chapel which probably existed as early as the 7th century. The body of the king, who was canonized in 1163, rests in a chapel in the apse. In the 13th century another pious king, Henry III Plantagenet, had the abbey reconstructed in the Gothic style.

Henry VII enlarged the abbey in 1519 by adding a new **chapel** in the uniquely English "perpendicular" style. The tomb of Elizabeth I is here. The abbey took on its modern appearance in the 18th century when a pupil of Wren contributed the towers of the façade.

You can visit most parts of the abbey daily from 8.30 or 9 a.m. until 6 p.m., except during services. So unless you've come to hear the highly regarded choir, don't try to visit on Sunday. The ambulatory and the royal chapels are open at somewhat variable times, but the best hours are normally between 10 a.m. and 3 p.m.

Guided tours are available, but if you prefer to visit the abbey on your own you should start by admiring the majestic perspective of the **nave.** More than 500 feet long, it is broken only by a high rood screen. Of the many tombs dispersed throughout the abbey the most notable are in **Poets' Corner.** Here lie Chaucer, Browning, Dickens, Tennyson and Kipling as well as the composer Handel (a longtime London resident though of German origin). The Tomb of the Unknown Soldier is also in the abbey.

You can also visit the **Great Cloisters** (to the right of the entrance), part of the abbey as it was in the 13th and 14th centuries. The **Norman Undercroft** houses a curious collection of effigies of famous people—as exhibited to the crowds at the time of their funerals.

In the **Chamber of the Pyx,** an ancient chapel remaining from the 11th-century origins of the abbey, were kept the standards for all kinds of money circulating in the realm. The **Chapter House,** with its magnificent tiled floor, dates from the same era. Until 1547 it was the meeting place of the House of Commons.

In the abbey grounds on its east side, the well-known 16th-century St. Margaret's Church is the scene of many fashionable London weddings.

*Where kings are crowned and poets are buried: Westminster Abbey.*

Whitehall is the sober street of government buildings. Heading from the Houses of Parliament towards Trafalgar Square the Foreign Office is on the left, the Ministry of Defence on the right. Just beyond the striped-pants precincts of the Foreign Office is a dead-end street known to all the world: **Downing Street.** Every tourist seems to want to take a picture of his companions outside Number 10, the office and residence of British prime ministers. But this has become more difficult. Because of the throngs of tourists standing about waiting for someone important to arrive or depart, barriers usually keep the public away to give the government some peace and quiet.

**Banqueting House,** on the right side of Whitehall, was the scene of many ancient feasts. It is the last vestige of the proud palace of Whitehall built in 1622 for King James I by Inigo Jones. The magnificent ceiling paintings are by Rubens. One depicts the king's deification; another symbolizes the union of England and Scotland.

Across Whitehall, the Admiralty used to command the world's greatest fleet. Next door, the **Horse Guards** maintain their traditional sentry

## Ministers and Sentries

Leaving the Houses of Parliament you may notice Old Scotland Yard, an unobtrusive building which figures in many a detective story. Get set for a disappointment: the famous sleuths don't lurk there any more. London's police have moved to another building between Whitehall and Victoria Station. For old time's sake, the modern HQ is called New Scotland Yard.

posts. If you can penetrate the crowd of amateur photographers revelling in the colourful costumes, you can try to catch the eye of one of these frozen-faced sentinels, mounted on a statuesque horse. Nothing can move these earnest guards… not even the prettiest girls.

## The City of London

The oldest part of the capital is called the City of London, but when Londoners talk about "the City" they are usually referring to the commercial and financial centre of the metropolis. (A stroll through the streets here is enough to sense the atmosphere of high finance.) But, technically, the City of London is the area administered by the Lord Mayor and contains more than ticker-tape machines and tower blocks. Both the contemporary and ancient aspects of the City are worth a close look.

At first glance it would seem quite simple to plan a visit here. The two essential monuments —St. Paul's Cathedral and the Tower of London—are only a

*Left: police at "No. 10", Prime Minister's residence. City gent keeps up with news of the City.*

mile and a half apart. But there are other things to see: the Guildhall, Mansion House, Fleet Street (the newspaper centre), and the Inns of Court. Have a look at the crowds at Bank underground station around 9 a.m. or 5 p.m. as the commuters—many wearing traditional bowlers—surge in or out of the City. Half a million people work here, but the area has only 5,000 permanent residents.

## Trafalgar Square to St. Paul's

From Trafalgar Square you can easily reach St. Paul's Cathedral via the **Strand.** Along

with the Thames, the Strand is the traditional route of all the kings and queens of England. If your royal carriage isn't handy, take the bus. The top deck of a red double-decker is the best vantage point. The only sight you'll miss from the bus is **Covent Garden,** a delightful square by Inigo Jones dating from the 17th century, home of the Royal Opera House.

Farther along the Strand, at Aldwych, American-designed Bush House is the headquarters of the BBC World Service. The bus route continues to Temple Bar, at one time the gate to the City. The bus

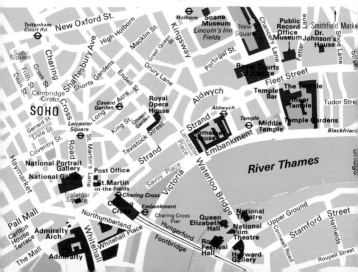

ignores this symbolic barrier but it's not so easy for the Queen when she arrives in her horsedrawn carriage. Like all the sovereigns before her, Elizabeth II on her official visits must ask permission to enter the City. By chance the Lord Mayor always seems to be on hand when he's needed, and each time—there's a good chap!—he grants the necessary permission. As a token of his obedience to the monarch, the Lord Mayor then hands over his sword to the Queen, who touches it and hands it back.

The Lord Mayor of London, incidentally, is the first citizen of the City but not of the rest of London. It's an honorary position. The Lord Mayor's Show, staged every November, is one of the most sumptuous and picturesque processions anywhere.

According to tradition, the heads of traitors were exhibited at Temple Bar as well as at the old London Bridge. But times have changed. The gate has been sacrificed to the gods of traffic jams, and Britain has abolished the death penalty.

But justice maintains a medieval tone in this area. Look around the **Inns of Court,** tucked away on either side of Fleet Street: The Temple, Lincoln's Inn and Gray's Inn. For

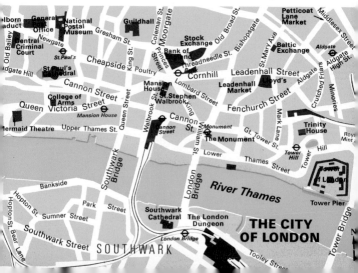

members of the Bar, the Inns of Court, oases of peace in the midst of the turbulent city, are a spiritual home. For the tourist though, the entrances are rather hard to find.

The **Temple** covers the 12th-century site of the headquarters of the Knights Templars. Middle Temple Hall dates from the 16th century. Temple Church, one of only a few surviving English churches with circular design, was built between 1185 and 1240. It was damaged in the Blitz, restoration work beginning in 1945.

As you go along Fleet Street you pass many major newspaper offices—the *Daily Telegraph* and the *Daily Express* on the left. Headquarters of the worldwide Reuters news agency is here, too. The press spills over into the side streets, where you'll also find some venerable old taverns. The whole district is animated day and night.

## St. Paul's Cathedral

Atop Ludgate Hill, St. Paul's Cathedral is the masterpiece of Sir Christopher Wren (see p. 40). Having worked on it for 45 years, Wren had the privilege almost always denied a cathedral designer: he saw his work come to fruition in 1710. He is buried in St. Paul's

in a modest tomb with the moving Latin epitaph: "Reader, if you seek his monument, look around you."

St. Paul's is the fifth church to be built on this site. The preceding one, an even bigger Gothic structure, was destroyed in the Great Fire of 1666. Some say that the earliest temple on Ludgate Hill was dedicated to the goddess Diana.

The present cathedral, inspired by St. Peter's in Rome, is chiefly remarkable for its **dome** (height 365 feet, diameter 112 feet). Its massive, grandiose appearance is somewhat relieved by a wide colonnade. The interior has perhaps fewer historical associations than Westminster Abbey, but it nonetheless contains the tombs of both Nelson and the Duke of Wellington. This was also the scene of the state funeral of Sir Winston Churchill.

Don't miss the **Whispering Gallery** under the dome. By some strange acoustical phenomenon, you can hear the slightest whisper from the other side of the gallery, more than 100 feet away.

From the dome of the cathe-

dral, all London spreads out around you. But first you have to climb those 727 steps. Notice all those tall modern office buildings—St. Paul's is the only historic building in the area, for it miraculously escaped World War II German bombs which devasted everything around it.

*In Middle Temple (left) two lawyers discuss a case. Right: Wren's masterpiece, St. Paul's Cathedral.*

39

### Two great architects

One architect gave London its body, another its soul. The soul is the work of SIR CHRISTOPHER WREN (1632–1723), whose delicate church steeples add such grace to the London skyline. Aside from St. Paul's Cathedral, he designed perhaps 50 parish churches. You could discover London by following the trail of Wren churches.

Curiously, this master builder was not strictly speaking an architect at all, but an astronomer. What set him a-building was the Great Fire of London, which began on September 2, 1666. By September 11, Wren had submitted a vast reconstruction plan to the king. The document has been lost, but its vision—realized by the buildings that remain—excites admiration among city planners everywhere.

The body of London—its most stately terraces and avenues—was the work of JOHN NASH (1752–1835). We owe to him the noble stretch from the Mall, up Regent Street and all the way to Regent's Park. No wonder that the style of Nash's famous terraces is known as "Regency". He combined all the elements of urban beauty into architectural unity.

Both lived to a ripe old age. Wren died at 90, Nash at 83.

# The City

Leaving St. Paul's, Cannon Street goes to the heart of the City, Europe's greatest business centre. Occupying only one square mile, the City seems confined to a small area, but its financial horizons are infinite.

Look at the people and try to guess what monetary melodramas are being staged today: the hurrying man in a bowler may have just bought several tons of Ghanaian cocoa on the commodities exchange; he's rushing to his bank to check on his credit resources. At the Baltic Exchange he'll learn that a ship already on the high seas can handle his cargo; at Lloyd's he'll insure it. As soon as he has a chance he'll re-sell the whole consignment to a Swiss chocolate manufacturer. And all this happens virtually on the same street corner!

"The world is our market" is the City's slogan. Britain may plunge deeper into debt, the pound sterling may be battered, industry may be in jeopardy, but the City goes on... happily making money.

This entire world of business hums along under the watchful eye of "the old lady of Threadneedle Street"—the Bank of England. In spite of the blind, bricked-up windows of this Greek temple with the look of a fortress, the Bank sees all and knows all.

Several other institutions of the City originated in the old coffee houses of the 17th century. The Stock Exchange, the Baltic Exchange and Lloyds, all developed from modest beginnings, over a friendly cup of coffee.

With overtones of spices, the open sea and adventure, the City is an exotic place to wander. Visitors are admitted freely to the **Stock Exchange** on weekdays, however, Lloyd's may be visited by appointment only. The Bank of England is, to say the least, inaccessible; even thieves have so far been unable to penetrate its walls. As for the rest, just take in the atmosphere of the streets and the pubs. This is where business is really a serious business.

Past the Bank of England, at the end of a blind alley called King Street is the **Guildhall,** the City's city hall. This beautiful building, constructed in the 15th century and renovated several times, contains some interesting rooms— among them the Great Hall in which the Lord Mayor is elected and a library with a rich collection of books, manuscripts and prints of London.

Not far from the Guildhall stands the monumental **Barbican Centre for Arts and Conferences,** housing multiple halls, theatres and cinemas, lending library and art gallery in a vast complex built on nine levels. This is the centrepiece

*Bank underground station at the heart of London's business and financial centre—the City.*

of a sweeping redevelopment project that includes tower blocks of flats and offices ranged around an artificial lake. Both the London Symphony Orchestra and Royal Shakespeare Company are based here in a move to revitalize the City's cultural life.

Opposite the Bank of Eng-

land, across the intersection near Bank underground station and the Wellington statue, stands **Mansion House,** a Renaissance-style palace from the middle of the 18th century. With its stately colonnade, this building is the official residence of London's Lord Mayor. Inside, the magnificent Egyptian Hall is used for receptions and banquets.

Nearby, in Walbrook Street, St. Stephen Walbrook is another of Wren's churches. The elegant dome was bombed out in 1941 but beautifully restored.

Finally, a monument by Wren you can hardly miss. It's called, logically, **The Monument.** This fine fluted column commemorates the tragic fire which all but wiped out London in 1666 (see p. 16).

King William Street leads to the Thames. Downstream lies one of the city's most famous landmarks, **Tower Bridge,** with its two towers and roadway that opens occasionally to let big ships go through. Between the towers is a glass-enclosed walkway: take the elevator up one tower, look at the view, cross the bridge and descend by the other.

*Tower Bridge walkway provides the finest panoramic view of the Thames.*

## The Tower

The Tower of London is a fortress constructed around the White Tower which William the Conqueror built in the 11th century. It has been a royal residence, a court of justice and later a prison—and therein lies its fascination, for many a horrible crime has been committed here. Among the celebrated victims: the sons of Edward IV, the Princes in the Tower, murdered in 1483 by order of their uncle, Richard, Duke of Gloucester. You can meet him in Shakespeare's *Richard III* trying to barter his "kingdom for a horse".

The father of the doomed children was himself no saint. He ordered the execution by strangling of his predecessor and cousin, King Henry VI, in a dungeon of the Tower. He also imprisoned his brother, the Duke of Clarence. Offered a choice of deaths, the duke jokingly opted to be drowned in a butt of malmsey wine. And so he was!

The list of the condemned is not for men only. Two wives of Henry VIII—Anne Boleyn and Catherine Howard—were also executed here.

If all this sounds too macabre for your taste, don't be put off. The fact is that except for the interminable queues the **43**

*World War II ribbons pinned to uniform, Beefeater guards Tower.*

Tower is a most agreeable spot. The lawns are green, as everywhere else in England, and a light breeze tells you the sea isn't far away. The fat ravens of the Tower are fed at public expense by a "Master of the Ravens" because of a prophecy that if the birds die out, the United Kingdom will disappear.

The interior of the fortress contains many interesting sights, by no means limited to relics of horror (like the headman's axe, famous swords and notorious dungeons). You can visit the charming 11th-century Chapel of St. John (said to be the oldest church in London); an astonishing **collection of armour** (of all sizes, fit for a child or an elephant); and the famous **Crown Jewels.** St. Edward's Crown, of gold, is so heavy that the sovereign only wears it for a few minutes during the coronation ceremony. Various other crowns are displayed, along with jewelled swords, orbs and sceptres, the whole lot set off by some of the world's most famous diamonds—the *Koh-i-Noor* and

**44**

the *Star of Africa,* for instance, and the ruby known as the *Black Prince.*

Stormed by more than two million visitors a year, the Tower of London is valiantly defended by about 40 men in Tudor costume, halberds at the ready. The Yeomen of the Guard are also known as Beefeaters. Amateur photographers can't get enough of them.

Every evening at 9.40 p.m. the Chief Warder presides over the seven-century-old Ceremony of the Keys. Solemnly turning a key in several locks, he closes the Tower for the night. To see this ceremony you need written permission from the governor of the Tower.

## The West End

How to define the West End? It's easier to say what it *isn't.* It isn't West London, which goes on for mile after mile toward Heathrow Airport. The West End is, in fact, a somewhat diffuse central district with these principal streets: Oxford Street, Regent Street, Bond Street, Park Lane and Piccadilly. On the west flank of the West End, Hyde Park serves as the district's lung, Soho and Mayfair are its heart.

The postal address of the West End—London W.1.—is so coveted that some people are willing to pay liberally for the privilege of a mailbox there. Yet W.1. laps over to the north of Oxford Street, where the character of the neighbourhood changes. And the West End theatre—London's Broadway—is not all geographically in the West End. For a Londoner, visiting the West End for shopping in the famous stores, seeing the latest play or film and dining at a distinguished restaurant is "going up to town". A town within a town, the West End is the focus for fashionable living, pleasure and dreams.

## Round the West End

For hardy hikers a tour of the West End might start from Tottenham Court Road underground station, heading west along London's busiest shopping street, **Oxford Street.** Huge department stores and smaller fashion stores and boutiques line this thoroughfare for more than a mile to Marble Arch. This triumphal arch of white marble was originally intended as an entrance to Buckingham Palace but moved here for some reason now forgotten.

Turn left into **Park Lane,** no longer a lane at all but a very busy boulevard with mansions and elegant hotels on one side and the eastern border of Hyde Park on the other. At **Hyde Park Corner,** turn left into **Piccadilly,** an important traffic artery known for its private clubs, discotheques and luxury shops. After Piccadilly crosses Bond Street, you come to Burlington House, home of the Royal Academy of Arts. Just a short way further east and you're in the middle of London's most celebrated traffic circle, **Piccadilly Circus.**

With its fountain presided over by a statue of Eros, Piccadilly Circus is a principal symbol of London. This intersection is so well-known from postcards and movies that it must be considered something of a masterpiece. But the truth is—and the urban development authorities agree—that this legendary place has degenerated into a "neon slum". Nonetheless, Londoners are so attached to it that they've indignantly rejected many attemps to change the face of the Circus. At night, with the signs glowing, it really can be exciting. And by any standard, the view *from* Piccadilly Circus up along the majestic curve of

**WEST END**

**Regent Street** (a triumph of John Nash, the visionary 19th-century city planner) is a wonder of harmony and stately grandeur.

From Piccadilly Circus, Coventry Street leads to Leicester (pronounced Lester) Square, home of some of London's most important cinemas. Then you can take Charing Cross Road, lined with fascinating bookshops, back to the starting point, Tottenham Court Road tube station.

To the northeast (landmarked by the Post Office Tower) is the district which evokes memories of London's early 20th-century literary life, Bloomsbury. There are many pleasant squares and two internationally renowned institutions—the **British Museum** (see p. 62) and the University of London. Farther east, at 48, Doughty Street, you can visit Dickens' House, where the novelist completed *Pickwick Papers* and wrote *Oliver Twist*. Dickens lived in several parts of London but this is the only house of his still standing.

*Oblivious to traffic noise and fumes, young visitors convene below Eros in Piccadilly Circus.*

## Soho and Mayfair

For more leisurely sightseeing in the West End you might prefer to take a bus along Oxford Street or Park Lane, with a break here or there for a pub or restaurant. But you still have to explore two West End "villages"—Soho, extending roughly from Charing Cross Road to Regent Street and Mayfair, between Regent Street and Park Lane.

**Soho** is a curious mixture of three elements: pleasures of all kinds (from gourmet restaurants to sordid nightspots), the clients who keep these establishments prosperous, and in the background, unsavoury characters, cashing in on any number of human frailties. Petty thieves and pickpockets mingle with the tourists and club-owners, but everyone is aware that if things got too

*Just off Piccadilly Circus, Soho is the place for bright lights; the hangovers can be theatrical, too.*

rough in Soho there would be no clients. So by and large you're relatively "safe" in Soho and local vendettas are usually settled quietly. At night though, be more careful in choosing the establishments you enter.

Just off Oxford Street, by contrast, peaceful Soho Square, a pretty 17th-century meeting place, isolates itself from all the excitement. Shaftesbury Avenue, farther south, is strong on theatres. As for Wardour Street, it might as well be Hollywood, British style: all the big names in the motion-picture industry have offices here. Two streets parallel to Shaftesbury Avenue, Gerrard and Lisle Streets, are the heart of London's burgeoning Chinatown —crammed with Chinese restaurants and shops.

So much for authentic Soho atmosphere. Carnaby Street, behind Regent Street, is not at all typical. Immensely fashionable at the time of the Beatles and Swinging London, Carnaby Street has suffered a certain decline, but it still draws throngs of tourists, particularly the young.

**Mayfair,** on the other side of Regent Street, offers the same pleasures as Soho, but they are more expensive and more respectable. Gambling flourishes

in specialized clubs; in some discotheques frequented by young jet-setters you may have to be vouched for by a regular client.

Mayfair is more varied than Soho. **Old Bond Street** glitters with fashionable stores, art galleries, fine antique shops, and jewellers attracted by the proximity of Sotheby's, the renowned auctioneers. Savile Row outfits the best-dressed men of affairs of the whole world. An unusual shopping **49**

*Dealers and art-fanciers mask emotions in tense auction at Sotheby's.*

gallery, the exclusive Burlington Arcade with its frightfully elegant little shops runs through to Piccadilly. Little has changed but the prices since the early 19th century when this pace-setting shopping precinct was built.

Elsewhere in Mayfair are beautiful 18th-century squares —Berkeley (pronounced Barkly) Square, St. James's Square and Grosvenor (pronounced Grove-ner) Square (home of the impressive American embassy building). Here you can still come across private houses manned by butlers and squads of liveried servants who seem to have escaped from the Victorian era.

Mayfair is for wandering, for enjoying the contrast between the teeming thoroughfares and the strangely quiet side streets, for quenching the thirst in any number of traditional corner pubs. Typical of Mayfair's surprises, Shepherd Market is tucked away behind the "skyscraper" Hilton Hotel. No longer a real market, Shepherd Market is a picturesque village square with boutiques and antique shops. The small houses here, some of them 18th-century classics, have plenty of charm—all most respectable. But when night falls, the narrow lanes of the Shepherd Market area are transformed into something resembling a red-light district. The inhabitants and the night prowlers seem to get along together and maintain quite neighbourly relations.

# Knightsbridge and Kensington

The residential character of these fine districts, south of Hyde Park, is more marked than in Mayfair; only the main roads are commercial. You can get some idea of who's who here as you watch the aristocratic horsemen taking their morning exercise on a famous path in the park called Rotten Row (the name may be an ancient deformation of *route du roi*—route of the king!). Here, even the dogs are thoroughbreds. But the neighbourhood is changing because of an influx of single people

and young couples renting furnished apartments while saving their money for a house with a garden in the suburbs.

South Kensington has more of a mixed population than Knightsbridge. North Kensington is cosmopolitan and Earl's Court, farther west, is so attractive for young Australians that Londoners sometimes call it Kangaroo Valley.

Here's a suggested route for exploring these pleasant districts of west London. If you start at Hyde Park Corner, follow Knightsbridge (the road) as far as Knightsbridge (the underground station). A bit farther along on the right,

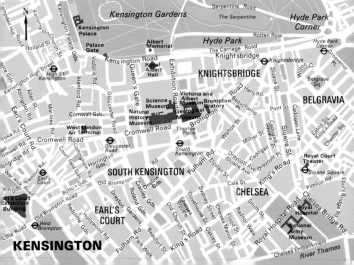

notice a big brick tower facing the park. This is the Horse Guards' barracks, a modern architectural success. The officers' mess is on the top floor, the stables on the second. You may see the surrealistic sight of horses peering out the windows quietly observing the traffic below.

Brompton Road, which branches off to the left at Sloane Street (a fashionable shopping street), is worth seeing. That Byzantine palace with the red stone façade, dominating the left side of Brompton Road, is London's most famous department store, Harrods (see p. 68). The adjacent streets are also interesting: Montpelier Square, one of the most charming in London, and Beauchamp (pronounced Beecham) Place, a fascinating shopping street with delightful old houses. Returning to the Brompton Road, at the next major fork in the road as you head west, the start of the

Cromwell Road is the site of four important museums: the **Victoria and Albert,** the **Natural History, Science** and **Geological Museums** (see pp. 64–66).

At the north end of Gloucester (pronounced Gloster) Road, you can enter Kensington Gardens, the beautiful western extension of Hyde Park. **Kensington Palace,** renovated by Wren at the end of the 17th century, was a royal residence from 1689 to 1760. It was the birthplace of Queen Victoria and is now the official home of Princess Margaret, the Queen's younger sister. See page 114 for palace visiting hours.

From there, if time permits,

*Londoners at work and at play: in a Soho street (left) and sailing boats at the Round Pond in fashionable Kensington Gardens.*

you can follow Kensington High Street with its fashionable boutiques. Or look at the mansions (some are embassies) in the private street called Kensington Palace Gardens, leading north to Bayswater.

If you're still fit you can hike back to Hyde Park Corner through Kensington Gardens and Hyde Park, an attractive walk but about two miles long (see p. 59).

## Chelsea and Hampstead

Though they're far apart, the atmosphere is similar in these two districts of London. In fact, Chelsea is often called the Hampstead along the Thames and Hampstead the Chelsea of the North. Both were once villages where travellers from London made their first stop on the road to the west (Chelsea) or the north (Hampstead). Though they've been absorbed into the big city they have kept their identities along with a village atmosphere. Both areas have attracted writers, artists and celebrated poets—Oscar Wilde and Mark Twain, Turner and Whistler in Chelsea; Keats and Constable in Hampstead. As for today's "starving artists",

they have long since disappeared from these expensive neighbourhoods.

Instead, you find today people who have succeeded in films, politics, journalism and the professions but without having lost the bohemian spirit. Nonconformism is often expressed here by a carefully studied relaxation in the sartorial style. The shops are very chic. One of them specializes in used jeans alleged to have been worn by real cowboys. In Chelsea, of course, they cost much more than *new* jeans.

To see **Chelsea**, start at **Sloane Square**, where the Royal Court Theatre was the first to dare to put on the plays of Samuel Beckett, John Osborne and Harold Pinter, thus launching the new wave of the London theatre in the '50s. West from there stretches the colourful King's Road with all the most up-to-the-minute fashions in the boutiques—and worn in the street. On Saturdays, the King's Road is one huge fashion show for way-out Londoners. One of London's big antique markets—the Chelsea Antique Market—houses

*A red-coated Chelsea pensioner watches fresh air enthusiasts drinking their beer outside a pub.*

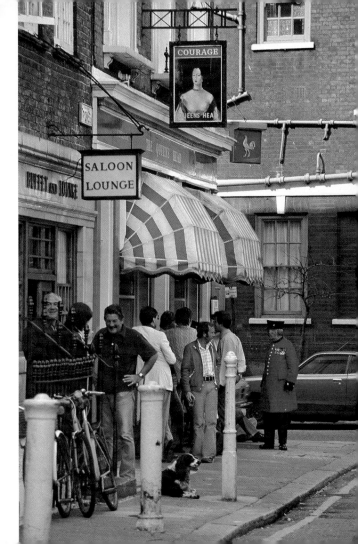

perhaps a hundred specialized boutiques. Throughout Chelsea you may see elderly but energetic men in age-old bright dress uniforms with three-cornered hats. These retired soldiers live along the river in the **Chelsea Royal Hospital,** a sprawling structure built, inevitably, by Wren in the 17th century.

Between the hospital grounds and the Chelsea Embankment, the well-tended lawns of the Chelsea Hospital Gardens serve as the site for Britain's most fashionable flower show every spring.

Farther west along the embankment, enclosed within solid walls, is the little-known Chelsea Physic Garden. For several hundred years herbs and other plants of pharmaceutical interest have been cultivated here.

Spanning the Thames a short distance upstream from here, the Albert Bridge is a graceful sight, especially when its night

*Flower-boxes, potted plants bring country closer to a quiet London mews.*

lights make it resemble a miniature Golden Gate Bridge. You can walk across it (but a sign warns soldiers not to march in step!) to Battersea Park.

**Hampstead** is also worth a visit if you have half a day to spare. You can reach the "village" on the underground. Because Hampstead is on a hill,

the tube station is London's deepest—192 feet beneath the surface. From the rough slopes of the magnificent park called **Hampstead Heath** (see p. 60) you can enjoy an absorbing panorama of London.

To the north of the Heath, on splendid grounds, is **Kenwood House,** a lavish neo-

**57**

classic mansion housing a fine collection of Flemish and English paintings. In the summer there are concerts here. The orchestra, on a peninsula in the lake, plays across the water to an audience in deck chairs. Sometimes it's hard to tell whether the trills are the work of a flautist or a nightingale. Hampstead has preserved some venerable inns, such as the 18th-century Spaniards Inn immortalized by Dickens in *Pickwick Papers*.

*Unofficial tourist attraction, man in medieval costume chats with admirer outside King's Road pub.*

## The Parks

What makes London so livable is the expanse of parkland. Within a six-mile radius of Piccadilly Circus, some 80 parks cover one-quarter of the city's area. It's impossible to imagine London without the relief afforded by its tiny green squares and vast public parks.

Londoners are at their best in the parks. See them on a Sunday morning, equipped with feature-filled newspapers they'll never have time to finish. Dutiful fathers are kicking a soccer ball with their children, dog owners exercising their charges, the wind wafting

kites and model sailboats. Everybody is "doing his own thing" without worrying about the neighbours. The spectacle of English freedom in action in a park is fascinating... and free.

Each London park has its own character—large or intimate, ordinary or aristocratic (ten of them remain the property of the Crown). All are pleasant.

**Hyde Park** is the best known, partly because of Speakers' Corner. This open space near Marble Arch echoes to unbounded eloquence, mostly on Sunday afternoons. Any orator who has a message—philosophical, religious, ideological, but rarely dull—can face the hecklers here. No theme is too controversial or outrageous to be aired at Speakers' Corner. A summer day inspires lovers to take a boat out onto the Serpentine (Hyde Park's artificial lake) or to stretch out on the grass, preferably near the bandstand when a military band is playing.

At one time **Kensington Gardens** was separated from Hyde

*Politics and religion—two principal themes for polemics at Speakers' Corner in Hyde Park.*

Park by a wall. In Victorian times only the "best people" were allowed in. Both the wall and the regulations on dress have fallen. Nevertheless, Kensington Gardens remains even today the more elegant extension of Hyde Park. Near Kensington Palace you can admire the Orangery and watch the children sailing model boats on the Round Pond, closely supervised by their nannies. To the south is an incredible neo-Gothic monument, the Albert Memorial, erected by Queen Victoria in memory of her husband.

**St. James's Park** was once swampland. Drained by Henry VIII and improved by Charles II and George IV, it is now an elegant park alongside the triumphant sweep of the Mall. The carefully planned expanses with their delightful perspectives lure not only tourists but civil servants and typists from the neighbouring ministries of Whitehall. You can see them enjoying a lunch-hour break in St. James's Park, munching an austere sandwich while meditating before the lake with its pelicans.

With its lake, canal, open-air theatre and zoo, **Regent's Park** is a favourite spot for Londoners. In the 16th century, Henry VIII used to hunt in the area. In the 19th century the Prince Regent, the future George IV, wanted to have a country house here. His architect, John Nash, designed a typical English garden in concentric circles and built the baronial terraced houses bordering the park. He also designed elegant Regent Street (named after the same prince), which extends from Piccadilly Circus almost to the park. But the country house never came to pass.

Don't miss the **London Zoo,** at the northern end of Regent's Park, one of the most famous in the world, where the animals are shown in a most attractive setting. Another highlight is the rose garden in the Inner Circle, part of a vast display of flowers.

**Hampstead Heath** is still a wild, natural bit of country overlooking the capital. The local residents are fiercely attached to the Heath; societies have been formed to buy nearby land to extend the borders of this unspoiled park. In summer there are concerts in the open air at Kenwood

*Hyde Park is crowded on a fine summer day. Sunbathers even go to busy Parliament Square (below).*

House on the northern edge of Hampstead Heath.

South of the river, **Kew Gardens,** in or out of lilac time, can be a pleasant and educational outing. Officially the Royal Botanical Gardens, 50,000 species of plants from all parts of the world are cultivated here. The greenhouses with tropical plants are especially remarkable and a fine park borders the Thames.

## Museums

London boasts dozens of top-rank museums, eminently worthy of studious attention. Picking your museums depends on your own interests and how much time you can spare. Here's a sampling of London's finest, beginning with five museums of exceptional importance. For readers' convenience, museum hours are grouped on pp. 113–115. Admission to nationally owned museums is free, but there are usually charges for special exhibitions.

The **British Museum** in Great Russell Street (Russell Square, Holborn or Tottenham Court Road underground stations) is one of the biggest and best in the world. The priceless collections, housed in a massive building dating back to the mid-19th century, are so vast that you'd be well advised to join a guided tour.

In the British Museum you can admire the celebrated friezes from the Parthenon. Known as the Elgin Marbles, they were appropriated at the beginning of the 19th century by the British ambassador to Constantinople, Lord Elgin, with the Sultan's blessing. As for the splendid Egyptian collection, it was snatched from Bonaparte after the Battle of Aboukir, in which Admiral Horatio Nelson defeated the French fleet in 1798.

The collection of prints and drawings is one of the finest in the world. You can see etchings and engravings, and watercolours and wood-cuts representing British and European schools from the 15th century onwards.

The museum also owns incomparable collections of Egyptian, Assyrian, Persian, Greek, Roman and British archaeological treasures, Eastern and Islamic antiquities and an outstanding numismatic collection. In addition, the British Library with its famous domed reading room, is a unique research centre. The manuscript collection is overwhelming—from the *Magna Carta* (1215) and a mortgage signed by

Shakespeare (1613) to the original manuscript of *Alice in Wonderland*.

The **National Gallery** facing Trafalgar Square (Trafalgar Square or Leicester Square underground stations) has been built up through gifts and legacies from private collections together with paintings bought by public subscription. The principal schools of European painting are represented by masterpieces of Leonardo da Vinci, Raphael, Botticelli, Titian, Rembrandt, Rubens, Velázquez, El Greco, Gainsborough, Hogarth, Reynolds, Turner and Constable, to name just a few. Only a part of the collection is exhibited; the rest may be seen in reserve rooms where paintings are hung in serried ranks, classified according to school.

The adjacent **National Portrait Gallery** shows nothing but portraits; generally the subjects are better known than the artists, though many famous signatures may be found. Special exhibitions are shown in the annexe at 15, Carlton House Terrace nearby.

*Among Greek antiquities in British Museum: Nereid monument façade.*

The **Victoria and Albert Museum,** familiarly known as the V & A, a museum of fine and applied arts, is in Cromwell Road (South Kensington underground station). Painting, sculpture, ceramics, furniture, weapons, musical instruments, clocks and costumes—with remarkable exhibits from the Far East, among others—fill 145 rooms with extraordinary richness.

The **Tate Gallery** in Millbank (Pimlico underground station) is small enough to cover in one or two visits. It contains examples of English painting from the 16th century to the present; don't miss the works of Turner displayed in several special rooms. An important section is reserved for modern art—a fabulous collection of impressionist, post-impressionist and expressionist works by Sisley, Cézanne, Gauguin, Matisse, Van Gogh and Picasso. There are sculptures by Rodin and Henry Moore. The museum is working towards expanding its contemporary collections.

## More Museums
**Madame Tussaud's** (Marylebone Road, Baker Street underground station). The ever-popular waxworks, a London tradition since 1802. A com-

*Portraits, may be for immortality, outside National Portrait Gallery. One of London's best modern art collections at Tate Gallery (left).*

bined ticket to the waxworks exhibition and the adjoining London Planetarium is available.

**Museum of London** (London Wall, St. Paul's, Moorgate, Barbican stations). London life and history from prehistoric times.

The **London Transport Museum** (Covent Garden, Charing Cross, Leicester Square). Full-size steam locomotives, coaches, buses, trams and working displays.

The **Science Museum** (Exhibition Road, South Kensington underground station). Shows development in science and technology and their applications to industry. From a replica of Galileo's telescope to modern rockets. The Wellcome Gallery shows the development of medicine. The adjacent **Geological Museum** contains minerals and gems of all kinds as well as a collection of fossils and a library with thousands of maps, photographs and volumes. Just next door, the **Natural History Museum** has collections of paleontology, zoology and botany. **65**

The **National Army Museum** (Royal Hospital Road, Chelsea, Sloane Square underground station). A new, austere building housing relics of army life from 1485 to 1914.

The **Wallace Collection** (Hertford House, Manchester Square, Bond Street underground station) is an old private collection, reflecting the taste of the Marquis of Hertford who created it. Among its treasures are French paintings of the 17th and 18th centuries, some fine French period furniture, together with porcelain such as that of Sèvres.

The **Courtauld Institute Galleries** (Woburn Square, Russell Square underground station). Contains some masterpieces of French impressionist and post-impressionist painters, and Italian painters of the 14th and 15th centuries.

*Visitors in South Kensington Science Museum peer at historic engine.*

The **Queen's Gallery** (Buckingham Palace). Temporary exhibitions which lift the veil on part of the fabulous collection of paintings, drawings and other works of art owned by Her Majesty.

The **Imperial Collection** (Central Hall, Westminster, Westminster or St. Jame's Park underground stations). Unique and authentic replica collection of crown jewels and regalia from many countries.

**Sir John Soane's Museum** (Lincoln's Inn Fields, Holborn underground station). Soane was an important London architect; he designed this house and lived in it until his death in 1837. He collected a treasure-house of English art (Hogarth, Reynolds and Turner) as well as works from antiquity.

**Museum of Mankind** (6, Burlington Gardens, Green Park or Piccadilly underground stations). Forms part of the British Museum and is particularly remarkable for its collections typical of the civilizations of Africa, America and Oceania.

The **Commonwealth Institute** (High Street Kensington underground station). The history, economy and culture of Commonwealth countries.

The **Imperial War Museum** (Lambeth North, Elephant and Castle underground station). Displays of weapons and equipment from the World Wars.

**Keats' House** (Keats' Grove, Hampstead, Belsize Park underground station). This secluded house, in which Keats wrote his dramatic *Ode to a Nightingale,* houses the poet's original works.

**Serpentine Gallery** (Kensington Gardens, High Street Kensington or Knightsbridge underground stations). Arts Council of Great Britain. Exhibitions of contemporary art.

**National Postal Museum** (King Edward Building, King Edward Street, St. Paul's underground station). Permanent and special stamp exhibitions.

**IBA Broadcasting Gallery** (70, Brompton Road, Knightsbridge underground station). Radio and television exhibition for amateurs. Guided tours to groups (max. 30).

The **London Dungeon** (28–34, Tooley Street, London Bridge underground station). Exhibition of British medieval torture, disease and witchcraft. Not for unaccompanied children.

The **London Toy and Model Museum** (23, Craven Hill, Lancaster Gate or Paddington underground stations). Victorian and Edwardian toys, model train collection.

# What to Do

## Shopping

Even if it bores you in other cities, shopping will delight you in London.

Having become the fashion capital of Europe, London keeps a step ahead of the rest of the world—possibly because no single style holds sway. Like most other aspects of London life, fashion is a live-and-let-live affair: wear what pleases you and never mind what people think.

One factor contributing to the pleasure of shopping is the soft sell. Nowhere in the world do the salespeople exert such low pressure. In fact, if you should hesitate between two similar items with different prices, the cheaper will probably be recommended.

For a while, when the value of the pound slipped, London enjoyed the reputation of a "cheap" capital. This, alas, is no longer true, and you have to look around, more and more carefully, and longer to find bargains. But they *do* exist. And you can use shopping as a pleasurable pretext for getting to know the city and people.

### Opening hours

As a general rule, stores are open from 9 a.m. to 5.30 or 6 p.m. non-stop. Some districts have late closing hours one night a week. In Knightsbridge, Sloane Square and the King's Road the shops stay open every Wednesday until 7 p.m. Oxford Street, Regent Street and Kensington High Street choose Thursday. (The late nights proliferate as Christmas approaches.) In the West End and the City stores generally close on Saturday afternoons. And everywhere the stores close all day on Sundays.

### Where to Shop

Before you set forth aimlessly, remember that some London stores are worth visiting as sightseeing attractions, even if you don't plan to buy anything.

In the luxury class, **Harrods** in Knightsbridge supplies the royal family and the aristocracy of Britain and many other countries. Watch the taxis and Rolls Royces depositing fashionable clients at Harrods' door. Inside this vast store, one department is more eye-popping than the next. Among the most spectacular are the food halls with their enticing displays of the world's best produce and the music department, where you can test all the grand pianos before buying one.

**Fortnum & Mason** in Piccadilly serves the same sort of clientele as Harrods. Here you can buy a jar of marmalade or a box of tea-bags from a salesman in a frock coat. English tea is celebrated on the premises every afternoon; you needn't be intimidated by the formality.

**Liberty & Co.,** in an extraordinary building fronting Regent Street, also offers a spectacle of luxury and refinement; noted for original silk prints.

**Asprey,** in Bond Street, specializes in gold, silver and leather goods.

**Dunhill,** in Jermyn Street, with its famous pipes and lighters, is in the same class.

**The Design Centre,** in the Haymarket, deserves special mention among the places for browsing rather than buying. Here a display of the latest British quality products shows ingenious advances in design

*No mercy for illegal parking, even for Harrods' aristocratic clients.*

and utility. Nothing is actually on sale, so there's no risk of succumbing to sudden temptation. But each item has a label indicating where it can be bought and for how much. A useful survey before your buying spree.

Turning from theory to practice, perhaps the best place to start shopping is Oxford Street. This is London's main shopping street, where you can find just about all the essentials at varying prices. (But if you prefer to avoid crowds you can find the same merchandise at the same prices in branches of the principal stores in suburban neighbourhoods such as Hampstead or Golders Green.)

**Marks & Spencer,** a chain of stores with a reputation for good quality and low prices, attracts hordes of buyers from all over the world; outstanding for sweaters of all varieties.

**Selfridges,** more imposing, has some 200 departments; among others is "Miss Selfridge", an immense department for girls' and young women's fashions.

Other neighbourhoods:

**Habitat,** in Tottenham Court Road and elsewhere, features elegant and modern articles for the home at reasonable prices.

**Reject shops** specialize in imperfect items, mostly porcelain and pottery. In spite of the negative-sounding name, the products are normally of top quality, generally the last of a series.

Toy shops: **Hamleys** in Regent Street is a department store for children of all ages and tastes. **Galt,** at the end of Carnaby Street, sells more "intellectual" toys for children under eight.

Another word on the subject of where to shop. In London one street succeeds another as the "in" place. Once Carnaby Street, parallel to Regent Street behind Liberty's store, was all the rage. Although the street is still there, and full of life, it has lost its original flair. Then there was the King's Road, with far-out styles which poured forth over all of Chelsea and the world—fashionable but transient. You really ought to visit the King's Road on a Saturday afternoon just to see the people. They come from all over, in the most outrageous outfits, pretending they live in Chelsea. Overflow boutiques are also found in the parallel Fulham Road. The latest outburst of fashion is bubbling in Kensington High Street, where boutiques and bistros are booming.

Most of these boutiques seem to do a flourishing business because they offer an attractive setting for selling fashions their young clients look good in. All of which rings cash registers more profitably than the old-fashioned system of forcing merchandise into the arms of the customer.

## What to buy

Visitors from the world over consider London shopping interesting, varied, frustrating, advantageous, mediocre or chic, according to taste and talent; you'll be rubbing elbows with Norwegian housewives and Nigerian businessmen, Kyoto teachers and Qatar oilmen. Oxford Street, for example, has become such an international shoppers' mecca that you can rarely hear English spoken.

For gifts or to take home for yourself you'll want to consider a whole range of British specialities from antiques to woollens. And don't forget such easily portable items as soaps, teas and tobacco.

Some suggestions:

**Books:** Serious bibliophiles will want to spend a day or two browsing along the Charing Cross Road; everybody else owes it at least a short visit. Big and little shops up and down this road have books on any subject you could dream of, and at low prices. Very strong on second-hand books and prints.

**Cars:** a bit cumbersome as souvenirs but have a glance at the local Jaguars, Daimlers, MGs, Bentleys and Rolls Royces, among others.

**China:** This is the home of Wedgwood and other highly coveted makes of china. Charming figurines and original designs.

**Clothing for men:** bargains in suits, raincoats, hats. Also economical in underwear. Or if you prefer, buy a kilt! Custom-made suits: the world's best-dressed men have their favourite tailors in Savile Row or Regent Street.

**Clothing for women:** traditional standbys are woollens—sweaters fit for evening wear or sheep-farming—and silks. Coats and raincoats are also good value. Note that the English have a special vocabulary for sweaters: jumper, jersey, cardigan, pullover, etc.

**Cosmetics:** All the international brands are on sale, plus fancy soaps in unusual shapes, colours and scents.

**Food:** The large stores have fascinating lines of British specialities so tempting you'll want to consume them on the spot. But they're packed to keep fresh until you get home: marmalades, biscuits and even cheeses.

**Games:** An astonishing range of clever games and toys for children and adults (see them also at the Design Centre in the Haymarket). London is a wonderland for toy soldier collectors.

**Replicas:** The bookshop in the British Museum (Great Russell Street) sells replicas of famous works of art on view in the galleries.

**Shoes:** If you can't find what you want in the shops—and the variety in style and price is immense—you can have them made to measure (Jermyn Street).

**Silverware:** The English style never goes out of fashion. Prices are interesting and the British alloy is purer than in Europe.

**Sports equipment:** With a huge population of sports enthusiasts, London's a good place to equip yourself for golf, tennis and, of course, cricket! Also terribly proper togs for horseback riding.

**Sweets:** The English not only have a colossal sweet-tooth for almost anything sticky and sugary, they also produce candies of great sophistication. Check out the mints, toffees, hard candies and lovingly packaged chocolates.

**Teas:** You've come to the right place to broaden your horizons on the traditional British beverage. Take home a box of something special from India or Sri Lanka, or mint tea, jasmin or a herbal brew to cure what ails you.

**Textiles and fabrics:** The British are still supreme in woollens, cashmeres, tweeds, etc. Buy them by the yard.

**Tobacco:** Connoisseurs far and wide know of two famous London shops—Dunhill and Fribourg & Treyer. They sell notable pipe mixtures and the best imported cigars. Snuff, anyone?

**What to avoid:** Because of heavy taxes, some items are cruelly bad bargains, unthinkable for your shopping list. Among the losers: cigarettes of any nationality, liquor, including Scotch and gin (except at duty-free airport shops), perfumes, cameras and electrical appliances.

*In a Chelsea store window, haughty mannequins model smart fashions.*

## Prices

The price of an article may vary considerably from shop to shop. You may find a real bargain in an establishment reputed to be expensive, while the same item shows up overpriced in a "cheaper" store. The only solution is to take time to compare.

Every July and January the big London stores hold their sales, causing considerable excitement among bargain-hunters. In some cases shoppers queue up all night on the pavement waiting for the doors to open, then suddenly lose their patience and good manners when the moment of truth dawns. In most un-British style, they hurl themselves upon the merchandise, incited by the chance-of-a-lifetime prices. During the sales—at least the first day—the pleasure of shopping is indeed limited to grabbing a bargain. If you plan to plunge in, be sure you know in advance what you want to buy and memorize the equivalent English sizes (see p. 106)—nobody will have the time to measure you in the general crush and confusion.

VAT (value-added tax) is charged on all retail sales, but if you intend to take a major purchase out of Britain you

can get an exemption (see MONEY MATTERS p. 117).

## Markets

You may not be planning to slip a Queen Anne chest of drawers into your luggage. Nor can you consume heaps of fruit and vegetables in your hotel room. But even if you buy little or nothing, London's antique shops and street markets are among the city's principal attractions.

*London can still offer real bargains. Cockney characters (below) buttonhole shoppers for charity.*

All the markets are interesting as a mirror of everyday life. Some, however, deserve a special visit.

**Smithfield Market** (Charterhouse Street, Farringdon or Barbican underground station) starts early (5 a.m.). This is one of the largest meat markets in the world. It might make you a vegetarian, at least for a day or two.

Still in the City, **Leadenhall Market** (Bank or Monument underground station) is a more appetizing sight. This retail meat and poultry market operates during normal trading hours under a fine Victorian glass roof between Leadenhall Street and Lime Street.

**Covent Garden,** halfway between the City and the West End, used to be the traditional market for fruit and vegetables. The heroine of Shaw's *Pygmalion* (and the musical *My Fair Lady)* was a flower girl at Covent Garden. After the transfer of the market to the south bank of the Thames, at Nine Elms, the Covent Garden area became the site of an ambitious urban redevelopment project. Now it's one of London's most popular neighbourhoods, with scores of small food shops, boutiques, gift shops and restaurants. The old fruit and vegetable market has been converted into a vast shopping arcade, and the former flower market now houses the London Transport Museum (see p. 65).

Even Soho has its market, in **Berwick Street** (Piccadilly Circus or Tottenham Court Road underground station). Daily except Thursday afternoons. As in the nearby restaurants, here you can find the freshest fruit and vegetables.

Near Petticoat Lane market (see p. 76) is **Club Row,** London's main animal market. Even if they can't take one home, children will enjoy watching the kittens, puppies, birds, goldfish and rabbits. (Only open on Sunday morning.)

### Antiques and Junk

Collectors of antiques and second-hand goods impatiently await the end of the week. It all starts on Friday with the **New Caledonian Antique Market** on the south bank of the Thames in Bermondsey Street (across Tower Bridge). The dealers arrive very early in the morning to stock up; by 10 a.m. they begin to pack up and go home.

Saturday is the day for **Portobello Road,** London's biggest, most colourful and amusing "flea market" (Notting Hill Gate underground station). This long road has a vegetable market in the middle, the junk market at one end and the antique dealers at the other. The bustle reaches its peak at midday, when the crowds of buyers, tourists, merchants and street musicians all seem to be having a good time together. Portobello Road is the place to buy more or less portable objects: silverware, candlesticks, pub mirrors, small Victorian boxes, old-time clothes. Though prices are not particularly low, you can try to bargain them down. In adjacent streets you'll find antique shops in which interesting discoveries can be made. Some, unfortunately, are closed on Saturday just when the Portobello Road is booming.

Choose Wednesday or Saturday for a visit to the **Camden Passage** antique market in Islington (Angel underground station), when open-air stalls are set up.

There is no such street as **Petticoat Lane,** but the market of the same name takes place every Sunday in Middlesex Street (Aldgate or Liverpool Street underground station) in the East End. This market, where you can find just about everything, is specially licensed for Sunday operations because traditionally there was a large Jewish population here. The salesmen of Petticoat Lane are noted for their sense of humor.

The **Farringdon Road Market** displays old books, manuscripts, etc.

## Antique Dealers

These are everywhere, even on the outskirts of London. They range from famous, elegant stores which sell veritable museum pieces to musty little shops heaped with bric-a-brac.

Prices vary greatly from one neighbourhood to the next, so take your time and compare.

All the big names in the world of antiques can be found in Bond Street, Mayfair, Pimlico, Knightsbridge or Chelsea. Their high prices are justified by the quality, rarity and authenticity of what they sell.

If you prefer unearthing bargains in more unusual, dusty shops, explore New King's Road (the western extension of the King's Road), or the streets adjoining Portobello Road, or Camden Passage in North London, with an indoor market and enticing small shops.

*Demonstration of ballroom dances fascinates audience in Hyde Park.*

# Nightlife

In almost every field of entertainment London is a world leader. You'll never have enough evenings for all the good theatre, music and night clubs. For an over-all picture of the entertainment scene, flip the pages of one of the specialist magazines, such as *What's On in London* or, more unconventional, *Time Out*.

Give top priority to a visit to the **cultural centre** on the south bank of the Thames. Since the opening of the National Theatre in 1976 this development has done for London what the Georges Pompidou Centre does for Paris or the Lincoln Center for New York. In an exceptional riverside setting, extending from Waterloo Bridge to the Hungerford Bridge (linking Charing Cross and Waterloo stations) are three fine concert halls: the Royal Festival Hall (3,000 seats and ideal acoustics), the Queen Elizabeth Hall (1,100 seats) and the more intimate Purcell Room, for chamber music. Here, too, you'll find the Hayward Gallery with its notable exhibitions of modern art, the National Film Theatre, a kind of avant-garde cinema club hidden under Waterloo Bridge, and the National The-

atre, which is, in fact, three separate theatres, forming a very British ensemble combining austerity and solemnity with popular appeal.

Even if you're not interested in music, art or theatre, go to have a look at the South Bank cultural centre. You might stumble upon a free jazz or rock concert, a poetry recital or an exhibition of paintings. The artists here "do their own thing", in good spirits but with conviction.

In the same line of country is the Barbican Centre (home of the London Symphony Orchestra and the Royal Shakespeare Company) in the City (see p. 41).

Incidentally, summer visitors have to adapt to the facts of northern life. In June and July sunset comes so late that nightlife begins long before nightfall. Conversely, in deepest winter a long lunch in London is likely to end in twilight.

## The Theatre

Speaking of a second Elizabethan period may be an exaggeration, but London certainly has shown great vitality since the '50s.

London's theatre world divides into the West End productions—the equivalent of Broadway—and the heavier fare of the Royal Shakespeare Company, the National Theatre and other, more "cultural" companies. In London it's not unusual for a play to keep running for several years. Musical comedies usually have the most longevity.

Avant-garde productions, often transitory and anarchic, may be found in various theatres of the "off-Broadway" type. The Royal Court Theatre in Sloane Square has a theatre club upstairs, the Round House in Chalk Farm puts on plays in an old engine shed, and the King's Head is a "pub" theatre (115, Upper Street, N.1.).

To avoid disappointment, decide at the start of your visit which shows you want to see. If you don't have the time or patience to make the rounds of the box-offices, a ticket agency will usually be able to get the seats you want—at a 20 per cent mark-up. (In some cases you have to exchange the agency's voucher at the theatre before the performance.)

If you're prepared to take whatever's going, there's a booth in Leicester Square selling half-price theatre tickets (open Monday to Saturday from 12 noon for matinées and from 2.30 to 6.30 p.m. for evening performances).

soft or hard drinks in the bars tucked away on different levels of the theatre. To avoid the crush you can order and pay for your drinks before the performance begins and they'll be waiting at half-time.

If you want a programme for the play you'll have to buy one. The usher who escorts you to your seat will sell it to you. But she doesn't expect to be tipped.

## Opera and Ballet

London's most beautiful theatre is the Royal Opera House, Covent Garden. Another well-known opera house, the Coliseum, is the home of the English National Opera Company (formerly Sadler's Wells). Among dance companies the Royal Ballet, the Ballet Rambert and the London Festival Ballet all enjoy great reputations.

British opera-lovers arrange their calendars around the Glyndebourne (Sussex) Festival every June. The rural setting is uniquely beautiful, the tickets are expensive and hard to get, and evening dress is *de rigueur*.

## Classical music

A large and enthusiastic public fills London's concert halls to hear major orchestras worthy

*Waiting for the show to start in top variety theatre, the Palladium.*

The audience's lot in Britain is brightened by the availability of refreshments before and during the performance. Tea is often served at the interval (intermission), or you can have

of a great musical capital. Outstanding are the Royal Philharmonic, the London Symphony Orchestra, the Philharmonia Orchestra of London and the BBC Symphony Orchestra.

Something you can't find elsewhere are the Proms (formally the Henry Wood Promenade Concerts), at which much of the audience enjoys the music while standing, often packed tightly together. This series of concerts enlivens the summer scene at the Royal Albert Hall, an incredible Victorian building which can hold about 8,000 people. It was world renowned for the bad acoustics; they said it was the only concert hall in the world where a new composition was guaranteed a second performance—thanks to the echo! But times (and acoustics) have changed—and for once for the better. Cheap tickets are available on the day of the concert for the promenade area. Proms are held from July to September.

All year round, chamber music, organ and choral recitals may be heard at lunchtime in a number of churches, notably St. Martin-in-the-Fields in Trafalgar Square, St. John's, Smith Square and the church of St. Stephen Walbrook.

## Jazz, folk and rock

For modern music of all kinds you can find a great variety of concerts at the Royal Albert Hall. Certain pubs, too, mostly on the south bank, specialize in jazz, folk or rock. The Hammersmith Odeon in west London is the site of Jazz Expo every autumn.

## Cinemas

Check the afternoon paper or the complete listings in *Time Out* or *What's On in London*. In addition to the major West End movie palaces, centred around Leicester Square, there are many cinema clubs. With few exceptions the performances are continuous. No matter how highly-priced and luxurious the theatre, the feature film is normally preceded by commercials, some of which can be quite amusing.

## Swinging London

It was Pope Pius XII who coined the expression, "the permissive society". But it was the English who put it into practice with the greatest enthusiasm. The meaning of the expression isn't totally clear. Is it the tolerant society? Or the indulgent, dissolute society? You might say that Britain has overcome its puritanism and extended its traditional tolerance to morals as well.

The results are paradoxical. Nudity has become commonplace on the London scene. At the opera, Cleopatra sings in her bath; Romeo and Juliet strip. But the strip-tease clubs are generally seedy. Homosexuals, both male and female, are represented by the Gay Liberation Front, with a hot-line service listing pubs, clubs and shows for those so inclined. Prostitutes have practically vanished from the streets, but they're easily found through small advertisements posted in certain shops, usually couched in terms of French models seeking interesting positions.

"Swinging London" might no longer be an accurate way to describe the capital. But you can see "Modern" or "Dancing London" anywhere young people congregate to do what they please. For insight, try to penetrate one of the fashionable clubs or discotheques in the centre or West End. Officially you must be a club member to be admitted, but some establishments accept temporary members. Others welcome any friendly face. Take a chance and don't be hurt if you're turned away. There's no shortage of addresses. **81**

# Calendar of Events in and near London

**January**
New Year in Trafalgar Square. Most untypically hilarious, with perfect strangers kissing in the street and celebrants diving into the fountains.

**February**
**Cruft's Dog Show.** Dog-lovers of the world and their pampered best friends at the pinnacle of canine competitions at Olympia for two days.

**March** or **April**
Oxford vs. Cambridge in the great **boat race** up the Thames from Putney to Mortlake.

**May**
**Cup Final:** Association Football's unrestrained climax at Wembley.
   A far cry from soccer, the **Chelsea Flower Show** is quietly colourful, a top social and horticultural event.
   **London Marathon.** About 16,000 runners participate in a 26-mile race round Central London.

**Summer**
The **Derby** horse race at Epsom in June is only equalled in prestige by **Royal Ascot** at Ascot (Berks) some weeks later.
   **"Trooping the Colour".** The Queen inspects her troops in Whitehall on the occasion of her official birthday, thoughtfully scheduled during the nice weather—the Saturday nearest to June 11. During the preceding weeks there are several colourful rehearsals, as majestic as the real thing, but without the Queen.
   **All England Lawn Tennis Championships.** The Wimbledon summit, last week in June and first in July.
   **Henley Royal Regatta.** In early July, in a delightful Thames-side setting, rowing and nautical competitions of a high level.
   **Kenwood Concerts.** Top symphony orchestras in lovely parkland every Saturday evening at 8 from June to August.
   **Royal International Horse Show.** Six July days at the Empire Pool, Wembley. Britain's No. 1 horse-owner, the Queen, presides.

**September**
**Last Night of the Proms** at the Royal Albert Hall. Concert with rousing audience participation, flagwaving, footstamping and singing. Tickets are so hard to get that queues start days, even weeks, in advance! Worth following on television, at least.
   **Farnborough Air Show** (alternate years). Spectacular acrobatics and a preview of tomorrow's aircraft at Farnborough (Kent).

**November**

**State Opening of Parliament.** The Queen in procession in the State Coach, from Buckingham Palace to the House of Lords.

**Guy Fawkes' Day,** the legendary fifth of November. Bonfires and fireworks commemorate the failure of the plot to blow up Parliament in 1605.

**Lord Mayor's Show.** A popular pageant, dating from the 14th century, celebrating the election of the new mayor.

**December**

**Christmas Carols** in Trafalgar Square nightly from December 15. And all over London, other reminders of Christmas Past and Tiny Tim.

**Christmas lights** are switched on from December 15 until January 6.

*No hard feelings: Morris dancers duel with sticks at a folklore show.*

# Sports

The British, who invented most sports, pursue them all with enthusiasm. In London there are clubs dedicated to the most varied sports, from tennis and soccer to mountain-climbing and ballooning. If you're involved in the same pursuits you may be able to become a temporary member.

For some sports you don't have to belong to a club to participate. If you're a swimmer, all you have to do is find a pool (for instance, at Swiss Cottage). For tennis, badminton or squash all you need is a partner and a reserved court. The charges and formalities are minimal.

Some London sports facilities are in themselves monuments of great renown. A shrine of **football** (soccer) is Empire Stadium at Wembley, where 100,000 spectators can watch important international matches and the Cup Finals. And soccer fans from Mexico to Moscow know all about Chelsea (housed at Stamford Bridge in the Fulham Road) or Crystal Palace in southeast London. A mob of English

*Wimbledon is summit of the tennis world. At Ascot (right) fashion shares the stage with horse-racing.*

football fans with its scarves, banners and war cries can be wilder and more spectacular than a band of Zulus.

The **tennis** equivalent is much more sedate. During the annual Wimbledon tournament the well-dressed audience makes it a point of honour to distribute applause equally action for so long, maintaining good spirits and even the occasional flurry of enthusiasm. Perhaps the explanation lies in the agreeable surroundings, the fresh air and the beer. Lord's Cricket Ground at St. John's Wood is the Yankee Stadium of cricket. But you can watch a more restful, inconsequential

among the players. Between games there's always time for strawberries and cream.

Some sports provide insight into the English way of life. The rules of **cricket** are not really as complicated as you might think. What is incomprehensible, though, is how the fans can sit and watch so little brand of cricket in any park or village green on any Sunday.

**Racing.** For the most elegant and important horse races, go to Ascot or Epsom, where you have a better chance of seeing the Queen than at Buckingham Palace. At less aristocratic tracks the fun is earthy. Colourful bookies chant the odds

*On Chelsea Hospital grounds, four
veterans revive sporting memories.*

while touts and other characters ooze amongst the crowds.
If you feel the need to bet on
a race and you can't get to the
track, you needn't feel left out.
Off-track betting shops operate
legally everywhere.

**Greyhound racing.** Wembley
(northwest London) and White
City (west London) are among
the top tracks for spending a
pleasant evening, having din-

ner, betting and above all,
watching the characters who
habitually go to the dogs.

**Rugby.** When it rains, this
gruelling game turns into a
mudbath. But after the final
whistle the players plunge into
a huge, communal bathtub,
singing lustily all the while.
This ritual is not open to the
public view, but the singing
sometimes continues at the
corner pub, with harmony by
former players, friends of players, fans and hangers-on.

# Wining and Dining

You can eat very well indeed in London—with a little luck.

Great gourmets sometimes ask how it happened that a country with the best game, fish and seafood could avoid producing a magnificent cuisine. The answer may be found in history and literature. After all, something must have happened to change the world of Tom Jones and all those epicureans and jolly-good-fellows into the much-maligned English cooking of today. Perhaps it was Puritanism. Or the Victorian era. Or the privations of two world wars. Whatever the cause, many English cooks admittedly have developed a rare expertise in the art of killing flavour.

Nowadays good English food is rarely found in restaurants. In the average London eatery you may be doomed to facing boring meat doused in an insipid sauce, accompanied by green peas and Brussels sprouts which have been steamed to death. For the best English fare you really need an invitation to a middle-class home where they still have time for cooking. (Some exquisite puddings and pies need months of preparation.) Or try the game pie in the dining room of an aristocrat—or of a poacher! Some of the nicest foods are regional (Lancashire Hot Pot, a tasty meat and vegetable dish, for example). The down-at-the-heels East End of London can still provide delights from an earlier day when people lived on cockles and mussels from the Thames estuary. Try the delicately smoked fish in any fishing port, or if you're exceptionally lucky, the Stilton cheese and port wine in the dining room of one of England's venerable colleges.

## Specialities

**Appetizers:** potted shrimps (small buttered shrimps preserved in a jar); fish pie (a very light fish paté); jellied eel; game paté.

**Soups:** oxtail soup, and from north of the border, Scotch broth (a thick mutton, barley and vegetable soup) and cock-a-leekie (a chicken soup strong on leeks).

**Main course:** The classic dish is roast beef and Yorkshire pudding. You may be surprised to learn that the pudding is really a lightly crusted batter designed to mop up the gravy—not unlike American popovers. Roast lamb in all its forms can be first-rate—often served with a mint sauce.

Game is popular. During the hunting season pheasant and grouse are prepared in interesting ways. Turkey and other domesticated fowl are usually served with a predominantly sage stuffing.

Steak and kidney pie is the most popular of a range of meat pastries offered in restaurants or, more frequently, in pubs. Others: Cornish pasty (pronounced pass'-tea—a turn-over filled with beef, potatoes and onions); shepherd's pie (oven-browned mashed potatoes atop a casserole of chopped meat, onions and carrots).

Main courses are usually served with cooked (often over-cooked) peas, beans, cabbage, cauliflower or Brussels sprouts. Potatoes—boiled, roast, baked or fried ("chips") —are inevitable.

Some restaurants specialize in fish and seafood of the highest quality—outstanding oysters, prawns, salmon and Dover sole.

**Desserts** (often called a "sweet" or, in some circles, a "pudding"). Ever since World War II sugar rationing was abandoned the British have been revelling in the sweetest of sweets. Vocabulary lesson:

a trifle is a sort of sponge cake smothered in sherry or brandy, fruit or jam, and custard or cream; a pudding is a flour-thickened fruit dessert, baked or steamed; and a fool is a light, tasty, refreshing cream dessert whipped up from a seasonal fruit. The most distinctive may be the gooseberry fool.

**Cheeses.** These are served after dessert. The king of English cheeses is Stilton, a strong, blue-veined cheese. Try some other English cheeses, too: Cheddar, Cheshire, Double Gloucester, Lancashire, Leicester or Wensleydale—all good, though you may find them a bit dry. A slightly creamier cheese, imported from Wales, is Caerphilly. The "latest" cheese is an English "blue Brie", Lymeswold.

Cheese is usually eaten with biscuits (crackers), which often have a somewhat sweet taste. If you prefer bread, ask for it —but remember that standard English ready-cut slices are often tasteless.

## Foreign Food

In London you'll have the chance to sample an impressive range of foreign foods authentically prepared to satisfy the most demanding and sophisticated tastes. Because London is so cosmopolitan, it boasts restaurants of every major cuisine in the world and some remarkable minor varieties.

Indian, Chinese and Greek restaurants merit special attention because they're not only very good but often quite inexpensive. Indian restaurants—along with Pakistani and Bangladeshi eating places —may be found all over the city. Greek restaurants are also widely distributed (just keep an

*Eurocuisine: French wine with British steak and kidney pie.*

ear open for the sound of the *bouzouki*) but strongest in Soho. London's Chinatown is just south of Shaftesbury Avenue, along Gerrard and Lisle streets…jammed with good (mostly Cantonese) Chinese restaurants as well as Chinese supermarkets and other shops.

If these cuisines seem too exotic, don't give up. You can easily find authentic German *sauerbraten,* Hungarian goulash, Japanese *yakitori,* Jewish dumpling soup, Middle Eastern *mezze,* Polish pickles, Portuguese *bacalhao,* Scandinavian open sandwiches, Spanish *paella* and Swiss *fondue.* Even homesick Americans are catered to: hamburgers, pizzas and ice-cream sundaes.

French-style restaurants are found in many areas of London. Gourmets from France dismiss most of them as inadequate, but a few of the best (and most expensive) are quite up to world standards. Italian restaurants proliferate in London. Some may be mere imitations of the original, but at least they tend to be more economical than their French counterparts.

Finally, vegetarians are well served, not only with snackbars strong on carrot-juice but some gourmet restaurants, as **90** well. All in all, you need never suffer from monotony on the gastronomic rounds in London.

### Helpful hints

In all good restaurants it's wise to book a table by telephone; on Friday and Saturday evenings it's essential. Other days, even if you arrive to find the restaurant half empty, you'll be more warmly welcomed for having reserved first.

Value-Added Tax (VAT) is included in all bills. A service charge of between 10 and 15 per cent is often added, as well. Even so, it's customary to leave an additional tip if you feel you were well served; the amount is left to your discretion.

What with big breakfasts and big dinners, you may find the only way to survive the rigours of sightseeing is to keep your lunches light. No problem: you can take your choice of snack bars, sandwich bars, hamburger places or pubs. You can also get good, cheap lunches in the big department stores. For a takeaway lunch, don't forget fish and chips wrapped in newspaper.

*In top London restaurant, master chef poses with his achievements.*

This grand old British dish, so often an object of fun or disdain among the unenlightened, can be a most delicious repast. It's cheap and nutritious, too. Fillets of cod, plaice, haddock or hake, covered in a rich batter, are deep-fried along with the potatoes. The clients add their own seasoning —mostly salt and vinegar.

Unfortunately, bad English restaurants and cafés are all too common. Watch out for restaurants advertising "3 courses, 3 veg." for a fixed price. You may be offered baked beans on toast or recycled spaghetti (often on toast!) or other grim inventions.

*Women beer-drinkers outnumber men at pub in Beauchamp Place.*

### Breakfast and Tea

Perhaps the best times of day for English food are first thing in the morning and late afternoon.

Breakfast begins with a strong cup of tea, often consumed before you get out of bed. When you finally get to the breakfast table, tea is liable to be replaced by coffee, an increasingly popular beverage in Britain. The famous English breakfast may consist of fruit juice, cereal, eggs (poached, boiled or fried) often with bacon (resembling Canadian bacon) or sausages and fried tomatoes. Kippers (a variety of smoked herring) are re-served for experienced stom-achs. Along with this goes toast —the English prefer it cold and dry—and marmalade. No won-der that breakfast is one of the highlights of English life.

Afternoon tea is a ceremony calling to mind the good old days. It's a pleasure that the English are now able to enjoy only at the weekend or during their vacations. You can take high tea in a traditional Lon-don hotel or, better still, on the lawn of an old country inn after a day's excursion.

Tea is served according to a ritual involving three courses. First come little sandwiches freshly cut into triangles, con-taining a thin helping of cu-cumber, ham, tomato or cheese. Next scones (biscuits) or crum-pets (muffins) are served, to be spread with butter or straw-berry jam and Cornish or Devonshire cream. Finally come the biscuits (cookies), jam tarts and fruit cakes. If you're very lucky all these ele-ments will be home-made and served by a couple of charming old ladies. Incidentally, the English put milk (never cream!) into the cup *before* pouring the tea.

## Drinks

The English have become much more worldly in their drinking habits. Alongside the beer-drinker in a pub you're likely to see someone reviving memo-ries of a holiday abroad with a French or Italian aperitif. Wine with dinner and cognac afterwards is the order of the evening in the better restau-rants. In fact, the great scope of the wine list—French, Ger-man, Spanish, Portuguese, Italian and perhaps Yugo-slavian and Hungarian wines— may overwhelm you. When in doubt, consult the wine waiter.

Mineral water is available in a few restaurants. Normally plain tap water will be served if you request it; getting ice can be a problem.

As for alcoholic beverages, the range of English favourites is broad. Before dinner, the traditional Spanish (or Cyp-riot) sherry competes with Campari or Pernod. For se-rious pub drinking there's Scotch from north of the bor-der (simply ask for whisky) and another very British drink, gin and tonic.

Beer, in many forms, is taken most seriously. Bitter is the biggest-seller, drawn from the tap into a non-decimalized half-pint or pint tankard. Other British brews worth in-

## London's Pubs

In the public houses (universally abbreviated "pubs") the English show their true faces. They're more relaxed, open and talkative. Perhaps this is why a foreigner sometimes feels intimidated, as if he were intruding on a family gathering.

Most pubs are divided into sections catering to different sorts of clients, with separate doors to the street. The public bar, where the chaps play darts and shove-ha'penny is noisier and cheaper than the saloon bar, which is better decorated and more sedate.

A few pointers on pub protocol: Never try to attract the barman's attention by snapping fingers, tapping a coin on the bar, or otherwise acting un-British; a smile is more effective. Pay for your drinks as they arrive. Never tip in a pub; however, it's quite acceptable to offer the barman or barmaid a drink.

By law pubs open for limited hours. There will be variations, but normal hours in London are 11 a.m. to 3 p.m. and 5.30 to 11 p.m., Monday to Saturday, and noon to 2 p.m. and 7 to 10.30 p.m. on Sundays.

Children are never permitted inside any pub.

vestigating: mild, which is reddish-brown and rather sweeter than bitter; porter, which is dark and heavy; and stout, heavier still due to its high hop content. Ale is much like beer, but brewed at a higher temperature with more rapid fermentation. Lager resembles American and European beers.

**94**

Apple cider is another popular drink for the thirsty days. Warning: in England this refreshing drink has a high alcohol content.

A final word about tea. In cheap restaurants and cafés the clients sometimes drink tea with their meals. This is frowned upon in more sophisticated circles. As a rule tea is only consumed *between* meals —very strong and very often. After (not during) dinner the British usually drink coffee, not tea. If the flavour of English coffee, boiled and re-boiled, is not exactly your cup of tea, you can find relief in one of the many espresso coffee bars.

*With his pint of bitter poised, pub client chats up the barmaid.*

# London for Children

To keep the children amused, the best London fun is afloat. Take a boat to somewhere like Windsor or Greenwich, enjoying the fresh air and shipboard excitement while you travel.

Aside from sightseeing on the Thames (take your camera for new angles on Big Ben or St. Paul's), there are historic ships to visit. H.M.S. *Belfast*, moored opposite the Tower, saw plenty of action in World War II. In St. Katherine's Dock, near Tower Bridge, you can go aboard *Discovery*, Captain Scott's polar-exploration ship. At Greenwich, two fascinating boats are on view: the *Cutty Sark*, a 19th-century freighter, and *Gypsy Moth IV*, which Sir Francis Chichester single-handedly sailed around the world.

The aptly named London district of Little Venice is the place to go for boat or barge trips along Regent's Canal; one route goes to the zoo. Incidentally, a special children's zoo in Regent's Park has pony rides and small animals to cuddle.

A final seafaring suggestion: you can hire a sailing boat or at least a rowing boat and ply the waters of the Serpentine in Hyde Park.

For youngsters interested in more modern means of transport, London Airport (Heathrow) offers all the excitement of constant landings and takeoffs by planes of many nations. View from the roof of the Queen's Building.

For rainy days, museums of special interest to children (in addition to those listed earlier in this book):

**Bethnal Green Museum,** Cambridge Heath Road, E.C.2—18th- and 19th-century toys, dolls, dolls-houses and costumes.

**Pollock's Toy Museum,** 1, Scala Street, W.1. Old toys, puppets, dolls.

Now some seasonal events, if you happen to be in London at the right time.

**January:** International boat show at Earl's Court; Londoners try to escape winter with thoughts of tropical seas.

**July:** Royal Tournament, also at Earl's Court—a military spectacle with colour, music and unusual competitions.

**December:** Pantomimes, those distinctively British Christmas-time shows for children; musicals on fairy-tale themes, featuring top comics and pop stars (often continue on into January).

And if all else fails, you can always take the children to Trafalgar Square to feed the pigeons.

# Excursions

At the weekend you may want to follow the Londoners out of town.

**Greenwich** (about 7 miles downriver from Charing Cross). The National Maritime Museum is in the 17th-century Queen's House, designed by Inigo Jones. The Observatory, in a park designed by Louis XIV's landscape architect, Le Nôtre, is the home of Greenwich Mean Time and zero longitude. Don't miss the fine painted hall in Greenwich Hospital, and see also the *Cutty Sark* and *Gypsy Moth IV*.

**Hampton Court** (about 12 miles southwest of London). Hampton Court Palace was built in the 16th century by Cardinal Wolsey, enlarged by Henry VIII and partly reconstructed under the direction of Wren in the 18th century. The State Apartments house a fine collection of paintings, tapestries, furniture and weapons. In the Great Hall the ceiling is a triumph of wood-carving. The beautiful gardens include several curiosities: living grapevines more than two centuries old; a 16th-century tennis court, and the famous Maze, a labyrinth of shrubbery in which you just might get lost.

*Excursionists fan out at Hampton Court, Henry VIII's country home.*

**Windsor and Eton** (about 21 miles west of London). Windsor Castle, begun in the 11th century and reconstructed and modified until the 19th century, is by any standards an overpowering royal residence. From the Round Tower you enjoy a masterful view over the surrounding countryside. Outstanding sights in the State Apartments include great drawings by Rembrandt, Michelangelo, Leonardo da Vinci, and Queen Mary's doll's house. St. George's Chapel, built in the 15th century, is the mother church of the Order of the Garter.

Eton, a nearby town, is best known for its College, founded in 1440 by Henry VI. The scholars, in their traditional black gowns, are among the unique sights on the campus.

**Oxford\*** (about 60 miles west of London). You can visit all 34 colleges in this town which is so rich in monuments. Magnificent

*With military precision bandsmen at Windsor keep up with the score.*

buildings line two famous streets known as "The High" and "The Broad". Magdalen (pronounced Maudlin) College, founded in 1458, is marked by a Gothic clock tower. Christ Church College was founded in 1525; see Christ Church Cathedral, dating from the 12th century, and Tom Tower, built by Wren in 1681–2 and containing the bell known as Great Tom. Could British understatement explain why one of the oldest colleges in Oxford (1379), is named New College? The 15th-century Divinity School has a magnificent vault restored by Wren. The Bodleian Library (15th century) in Radcliffe Square is one of the world's oldest and finest. Oxford's Ashmolean Museum is strong on archaeological remains, medieval art and English, Dutch, French and Italian painting. In Broad Street the Sheldonian Theatre is one of Wren's first works (17th century).

**Cambridge** (about 55 miles north of London). With ex-scholars from Sir Isaac Newton to Bertrand Russell, Cambridge has a record of academic brilliance hard to beat. Colleges range from Peterhouse (1284) to modern faculties of science and technology. The University Library receives a copy of every book printed in the United Kingdom and has over 2½ million volumes. Walk among the predominantly grey stone buildings of the town. See King's College Chapel, an outstanding example of late-Gothic architecture; Pembroke College Chapel (1665), Wren's first completed building; Trinity College (founded by Henry VIII), the largest in Cambridge, and Queen's College, housed in a picturesque set of medieval buildings. Don't miss the Fitzwilliam Museum's collections of coins and medals, paintings and prints—and for relaxation, try punting (propelling a long, flat-bottomed boat with a pole) on the river Cam.

**Stratford-on-Avon\*** (about 85 miles northwest of London). Shakespeare's birthplace is a top tourist attraction, but it's difficult to get to. For an easy pilgrimage, take an organized coach tour. The house in which Shakespeare was born (1564), in Henley Street, contains quaint old furniture and interesting manuscripts. Visit Holy Trinity Church where he was baptised and buried, Hall's Croft, where his daughter Susanna lived, and Anne Hathaway's cottage, a thatched cottage in which Shakespeare's wife lived before their marriage. Elsewhere in town: the medieval Clopton Bridge, near the poet's statue and some fine old inns, such as The Falcon and The Shakespeare. In the modern Royal Shakespeare Theatre the bard's works are performed from March to December. The building also contains a museum and picture gallery.

---

\* For a complete guide, purchase the Berlitz travel guide OXFORD AND STRATFORD.

# How to Get There

Although the fares and conditions described below have all been carefully checked, it is advisable to consult a travel agent for the latest information on all arrangements.

## BY AIR

### From North America

**Scheduled Flights:** major airlines throughout the United States and Canada offer frequent service to London, and there are nonstop flights (daily in many cases) from over 20 cities, including Vancouver, Montreal, Toronto, Houston, Chicago, Los Angeles, Miami, Washington and New York.

In addition to first class and economy rates, neither of which require advance purchase of tickets, there are a number of excursion fares available. The least expensive of these are *APEX* (Advance Purchase Excursion) and Super-*APEX*. The *APEX* fare must be reserved and paid for 30 days in advance of departure and is valid for a trip of 7 to 180 days. One stopover is permitted for an additional charge, and there is a penalty if you cancel. Super-*APEX* must be reserved 21 days in advance and is good for a period of 7 to 180 days, though no stopovers are allowed and your money is not refunded in case of cancellation. There are lower cost fares available, but in general from New York only. These are the one-way *Standby Fare* sold on a first-come, first-served basis only when seats are available, and the *Budget Fare* for which full payment must be made at least 21 days before the first day of the week in which you're travelling.

**Charter Flights and Package Tours:** Your travel agent can give you information about the availability of One-Stop Inclusive Tour Charters (OTC) and Advance Booking Charters (ABC). The OTC must be paid for 30 days in advance of departure and the less expensive ABC at least 45 days in advance. Land arrangements, included in the OTC ticket, are not necessarily a part of an ABC package. As with other bargain tickets, there is a penalty for cancellation of OTC or ABC arrangements.

### From Australia, New Zealand and South Africa

Apart from special charters, the basic types of fare available for these routes to London are as follows: *APEX* (Advanced Purchase Excursion) available from Australia for a one-year maximum stay (no minimum stay requirement). The *APEX* fare is also available from New Zealand (valid 21 to 180 days). These tickets must be booked 45 days in advance.

Then there is a *return excursion* fare (valid 21-day minimum stay to 270-day maximum stay for Australia and 21 days to one year for New Zealand). Finally there are two special one-way fares from Australia, *Economy Class One-Way* and *Advance Purchase One-Way*. The *Economy Class One-Way* fare need not be purchased in advance, while the *Advance Purchase One-Way* is subject to the same conditions as the *APEX* fare. This latter fare is also available from New Zealand.

South Africa also has an *APEX* fare (valid 14–90 days) as well as an economy class excursion ticket (valid 19–75 days).

## BY SEA

### From North America

Although its transatlantic schedule has been cut to about a dozen trips each way (April to October) between New York and Southampton, the *Queen Elizabeth 2* still offers travellers with the time and inclination for a voyage, the opportunity to savour an almost vanished experience, a crossing on a luxury ocean liner. Consult your travel agent for the current schedule.

More readily available (though on no regular schedule of departure) is the adventure of travelling on a freighter and you can choose a St. Lawrence, Atlantic or Gulf Coast port to travel from.

# When to Go

London is fun to visit in any season, although in mid-winter it can be wet, windy and cold. To compensate, you will find the metropolis less congested than in July, the museums open and the world of entertainment in full swing.

This table will give you a good idea of what to expect:

| Temperature | | J | F | M | A | M | J | J | A | S | O | N | D |
|---|---|---|---|---|---|---|---|---|---|---|---|---|---|
| maximum | °F | 45 | 46 | 50 | 55 | 63 | 68 | 71 | 70 | 66 | 59 | 50 | 46 |
| | °C | 7 | 8 | 10 | 13 | 17 | 20 | 22 | 21 | 19 | 15 | 10 | 8 |
| minimum | °F | 39 | 39 | 39 | 45 | 48 | 54 | 57 | 54 | 54 | 50 | 43 | 39 |
| | °C | 4 | 4 | 4 | 7 | 9 | 12 | 14 | 12 | 12 | 10 | 6 | 4 |

# Planning Your Budget

To give you an idea of what to expect, here are some average prices in pounds sterling (£). However, due to the annual inflation rate, they must be regarded as approximate.

**Airport transfers.** *Heathrow* to Central London, taxi £14–15, underground (subway) to Piccadilly Circus £1.50, "Airbus" to Paddington, Victoria or Euston via major hotels £2.50, Green Line 767 to Victoria £2. *Gatwick* to London, taxi £28–30, train to Victoria £3.

**Car hire** (international agency). *Ford Escort L* £19.75 per day including 200 free miles, 15 p a mile above that, £106.75 per week with unlimited mileage. *BMW 316* £33.50 per day including first 200 miles, 24p per mile above that, £173.25 per week with unlimited mileage. *Mercedes 230* £48 per day, 48p per mile, £490, with unlimited mileage. Add 15% VAT and insurance.

**Cigarettes.** £1.05 and upwards per packet of 20.

**Entertainment.** Cinema £3 and upwards, discotheque £2–5, musical £6–18, night club £3–12, theatre £3.50–15.

**Guides.** £28 half-day plus £2.50 for languages, £42 full day plus £5 for languages.

**Hairdressers.** *Women's* shampoo and set £4–6, permanent wave £20 upwards, manicure from £3.00. *Men's* wash, cut and blow-dry £5, trim £3, shave £2.50.

**Hotels** (Inner London, double room with bath). **** £70, *** £50, ** £20, "bed and breakfast" from £15 (plus shower from £20).

**"London Explorer Pass".** 1 day £3, 3 days £8.50, 4 days £11, 7 days £16 (children under 16: 1 day £1.50, 3 days £3, 4 days £4, 7 days £6).

**Meals and drinks.** English breakfast £2.50 and upwards, continental breakfast £1.50 and upwards, lunch £7.50, dinner £12 in a fairly good establishment, beer (pint) 80p, whisky 75–85p, soft drink 45p.

**"Round London Sightseeing Tour".** £2.95 for adults, children £1.50.

**Shopping bag.** Loaf of bread 47p, butter 55–60p, 6 eggs 40–45p, instant coffee (100 grams) £1.10–1.40, milk (pint) 22p.

**Taxi.** Minimum charge 60p for first 618 yds. (or first 2 min. 12 secs.), plus 10p for every further 309 yds. or 106 secs., 15p extra per passenger, £3.90 for first 6 miles plus 10p for every 216 yds. after that (or 44 secs.).

**Underground.** Central zone fare 40p, Two zone fare 50p, Three zone fare 80p, Four zone fare £1.00, Five zone fare £1.30.

# BLUEPRINT for a Perfect Trip

## An A-Z Summary of Practical Information and Facts

## Contents

A star (*) following an entry indicates that relevant prices are to be found on page 102.

**A**  **ACCOMMODATION\*.** See also Camping. London's tourist boom keeps the hotels full much of the time. If your accommodation isn't automatically included in your travel arrangements, better make reservations well in advance. Arriving in London on the spur of the moment, without a booking, needn't mean you have to sleep under the bridges, but you may well have to stay a long way from the centre. Hotel reservations can be made at the London Tourist Board centres (see Tourist Information Offices).

The **hotels** of London range from the most sumptuous to frankly spartan quarters. In the luxury class you have a choice between American-style establishments and traditional British hotels with service fit for a king.

**Bed and breakfast** ("B & B") accommodation is offered in many simple private homes and announced by a corresponding sign in the garden or window. Landladies like to keep regular hours and may impose a night-time curfew.

**Motels** are frequently found in or near British cities.

**Youth and student accommodation** is reasonably plentiful but, again, you're advised to reserve well ahead in summer. A sampling:

YMCA, 112, Great Russell Street, London W.C.1
YWCA, Central Club, 16, Great Russell Street, London W.C.1
YWCA, Victoria, 118, Warwick Way, London S.W.1
Baden Powell House International Hostel, Queen's Gate, London SW7 5JS
Central University Hostel, 7, Bedford Place, London WC1B 5JA
Gayfere Hostels Ltd., 8, Gayfere Street, London SW1P 3HN

The London Tourist Board's booklet *Where to Stay: London* is a very helpful guide to choosing a place to stay in the greater London area.

**AIRPORTS\*.** London is served by two major airports: Heathrow (principally for scheduled flights) and Gatwick (mostly charters). Two smaller and more distant airports, Stansted and Lūton, specialize in charter traffic.

Heathrow, one of the world's busiest airports, is located about 15 miles west of London. The "Airbus" A1, A2 and A3 express services, operated by London Transport, connect Heathrow's three terminals with the centre of London—A1 to Victoria, calling at Cromwell Road and Hyde Park Corner, A2 to Paddington, calling at Holland Park Avenue and Bayswater Road, A3 to Euston, calling at Hammersmith, Kensington High Street, Park Lane, Marble Arch and Russell Square. The journey time is 50 to 60 minutes. Green Line "Flightline" 767 runs direct from the airport to Victoria coach station in about 40 minutes.

The Piccadilly underground line to Heathrow provides a fast connection with all parts of London.

Taxi fares to and from the airport are controlled as in Central London—but that doesn't stop them from being high.

Gatwick, to the south of London, is about twice as far out as Heathrow, but travel is fast and convenient. A railway line runs between Gatwick and Victoria Station. Trains leave the airport buildings every 15 minutes during the day and take 40 minutes (minimum).

If you have to change airports, Green Line express coach 727 links Heathrow with Gatwick and Luton airports (No. 747 links Heathrow and Gatwick only). There is also a helicopter service between Heathrow and Gatwick.

Facilities at both main airports cover the full range: currency-exchange offices, free self-service baggage carts, porters, car hire counters, restaurants and bars, post offices, well stocked, duty-free supermarkets and tourist information centres.

**CAMPING.** No, you can't camp out in the parks of London! Once the big iron gates are locked, police and their dogs check the dells and thickets to make certain no one is bedded down. Inevitably, legitimate campsites are a long way from the city centre. For all details on camping within a 100-mile range of London ask the London Tourist Board (see TOURIST INFORMATION OFFICES) for the pamphlet *Caravan and Camping Sites for the visitor to London,* or contact the Camping Club of Great Britain and Ireland Ltd.:

11, Lower Grosvenor Place, London S.W.1; tel. 828-1012

**CAR HIRE\*.** See also DRIVING. Piloting an unfamiliar vehicle through London's heavy traffic tends to make a car far more of a hindrance than a help in the city centre. Quite apart from this, leaving it—let alone parking it—becomes more of a nightmare each year. It's advisable to rent one only for trips outside the capital.

**C**

To do so, from one of the many local and international hire firms, the general rule is you must be at least 21 years of age (and not yet 70) and have held a driving licence for at least 12 months. Virtually all the world's driving licences are recognized by the British authorities.

**CHILDREN.** In Britain children are not really integrated into general life as they are in some other countries, especially on the Continent. Only rarely are they taken along to restaurants, and they're excluded by law from pubs. Nor are they allowed as much freedom, generally speaking, as American youngsters: children are treated as children.

Universal Aunts Ltd., a venerable institution that sorts out problems from meeting children at airports to finding a dinner jacket on a Sunday, also provides a baby-sitting service:

Universal Aunts Ltd., 36, Walpole Street, Chelsea S.W.3

Otherwise try:

Baby-sitter Unlimited, 313, Old Brompton Road, S.W.3

**CIGARETTES, CIGARS, TOBACCO★.** If you're a smoker, take full advantage of your tax-free allowance on your journey here (see CUSTOMS AND ENTRY REGULATIONS). The prices of tobacco products in Britain are proportionally among the highest in the world, and foreign brands are even more expensive.

**CLOTHING.** London's weather isn't as bad as you might have been led to imagine. Still, don't forget to pack a light raincoat and something to keep off the evening chill, even in summer. In winter the humidity and wind may make you colder than the thermometer shows. Even indoors you'll need to wrap up: the English, great believers in fresh air and draughts, do not overheat their homes.

Social convention says that you dress as you please. Rare are the occasions when men are required to wear ties; only a handful of conservative restaurants retain restrictions on attire. You can go to the theatre in blue jeans just as well as in evening dress.

**Clothing sizes**

**Dresses, blouses, knitwear**

| Great Britain | 10/32 | 12/34 | 14/36 | 16/38 | 18/40 |
|---|---|---|---|---|---|
| U.S.A. | 8 | 10 | 12 | 14 | 16 |

**106** *Note:* Men's suits and shirts (collar sizes) are the same in Great Britain and the U.S.

**Post office hours:** Larger post offices are open:

from 9 a.m. to 5.30 or 6 p.m., Monday to Friday, from 9 a.m. to 12.30 p.m. on Saturdays

Smaller district post offices have shorter hours. The post office near Trafalgar Square is open until 7 p.m.:

24/28, William IV Street, London WC2N 4DL

**Poste Restante (General Delivery):** If you don't know where you'll be staying in London, you can have mail sent to you c/o poste restante. The most convenient way would be to specify the Trafalgar Square office (see above). (Take your passport or identity card when you got to pick up mail.)

**Stamps** are sold at post office counters and from vending machines outside post offices. Don't expect to buy them in shops, even in those selling postcards.

**Telegrams** no longer exist in the U.K. They are replaced by services called Datapost, Expresspost and Intelpost. Enquire about details at the post office.

**Telephone:** There are plenty of public telephones on the street, in underground stations, at post offices and in most pubs and restaurants. They take 5p and 10p coins.

*Payphones* are being introduced at strategic positions in central London and at airports, main railway stations, etc. They are indicated by a blue or red telephone receiver symbol on the kiosk. These operate with 2p, 10p and 50p coins.

*Cardphones:* Buy a card at main post offices, put it into the special cardphone telephones; it will tell you how much you have left to use for further calls. Cardphones are green or indicated by a green symbol.

The old, more usual system is uncommonly complicated and perhaps somewhat terrifying at first. The machine won't accept your money until the connection has been made. And at that very moment—when the other party is trying to say "hello"—the line is interrupted by a series of rapid pips. At this disconcerting signal you must push your coin into the appropriate slot of the machine. If it's immediately returned, as sometimes happens, the pips will continue until you've introduced another coin or the same one with a different amount of pressure. The repetition of the flustering pips a couple of minutes later will warn you to put in more money.

**107**

**C**   It's much cheaper to make long distance calls between 6 p.m. and 8 a.m. and on weekends.

You can call Europe direct from most street telephone boxes. From private phones—not from coin-operated ones—you can dial direct overseas also. If you want to telephone collect, tell the operator you want to make a "reverse charge" call.

If your call abroad is likely to be a lengthy one and you don't have access to a private phone, there's another solution: from the Westminster International Telephone Bureau, you can call direct some 90 countries worldwide and pay on completion of your call at a cash desk. Otherwise, you ring through an operator (but no reverse charge calls can be made from the Bureau, nor are credit cards accepted). This system also allows you to take advantage of the considerably cheaper weekend rates since the Bureau is open every day including weekends:

1, Broadway, S.W.1; hours are from 9 a.m. to 5.30 p.m.

By using it, you'll also avoid the hotel telephone surcharge that is becoming more and more widespread. Similar telephone bureaux exist at Heathrow (Terminal 3) and Gatwick airports.

The area code for London is 01; omit this, obviously, if dialling from within London.

Useful telephone numbers are listed in the front pages of the London A-D telephone book.

"Teletourist", a telephone information service for visitors, will inform you about the principal events of the day—phone 246-8041; for children's activities, dial 246-8007; for information on current exhibitions, ring "Dial-an-Exhibition", 730-0977; in French, 246-8043; in German, 246-8045.

**COMPLAINTS.** In Great Britain, consumer protection enjoys legal backing. If an article doesn't correspond to its description, or is defective, you may always return it (providing you've kept the sales receipt). Since the law is on your side, you'll have no trouble from the shop-owner. Though proprietors may offer you a voucher for the amount in question, you have the right to insist on a cash refund.

If you should have a stubborn problem with overcharging or bad workmanship, consult a local Citizens' Advice Bureau or the Consumers' Association:

14, Buckingham Street, London W.C.2; tel. 839-1222

**108** In cases of gross abuse, go to the nearest police station.

**CONSULATES.** All embassies, consulates and Commonwealth high commissions are listed in the yellow pages of the telephone directory under the heading "Embassies, Consulates, High Commissions and Legations".

**Australia:** Australia House, Strand, London WC2B 4LA; tel. 438-8000; hours: 9 a.m. to 5 p.m. Monday to Friday.

**Canada:** Canada House, Trafalgar Square, London SW1Y 5BJ; tel. 629-9492; hours: 9 a.m. to 5 p.m. Monday to Friday.

**Eire:** 17, Grosvenor Place, London SW1X 7HR; tel. 235-2171; hours: 9.30 to 1 p.m. and 2.15 to 5 p.m. Monday to Friday.

**New Zealand:** New Zealand House, Haymarket, London SW1Y 4TQ; tel. 930-8422; hours: 9 a.m. to 5 p.m. Monday to Friday.

**South Africa:** South Africa House, Trafalgar Square, London WC2N 5DP; tel. 930-4488; hours: 9.30 a.m. to 4.30 p.m. Monday to Friday.

**U.S.A.:** 5, Upper Grosvenor Street, London W1A 2JB; tel. 499-5521; hours: 9 a.m. to 1 p.m. Monday to Friday.

**CRIME and THEFT.** Violent crime is still rare in this enormous city, but you ought to be on your guard against pickpockets and petty thieves. Wherever crowds gather—for example at the markets of Portobello Road and Petticoat Lane—watch your wallet. Always lock your car when you park it, and remove all visible objects. Hotels advise their guests to lock up valuables in the hotel safe.

**CUSTOMS and ENTRY REGULATIONS.** See also DRIVING IN BRITAIN. Americans, South Africans and citizens of Commonwealth countries need only a valid passport—no visa—for tourist visits. However, careful checks are made on people entering for more than three weeks, e.g. amount of funds they carry with them, return tickets, etc., so entrants may have to face a barrage of questions. There are no passport controls between Eire and Britain.

The only occasion when you might need a smallpox vaccination is if you're arriving from an infected country. Other vaccinations are required only in exceptional cases. If in doubt, consult your travel agent.

Upon arrival in Britain you'll have to fill in an entry card giving your particulars and the address you'll be staying at during your visit. The immigration officer will stamp your passport permitting you to stay in Britain for a specific length of time. If your plans are uncertain, ask for

**C** several months so you don't have to renew your visa later. Provided you look reasonably respectable and have sufficient funds with you to cover your stay, there's usually no problem.

In British ports and airports if you have goods to declare you follow a red channel; with nothing to declare you take the green route, bypassing inspection. But customs officers look over the faces of green-channel travellers and uncannily choose certain tourists to check.

The following chart shows what main duty-free items you may take into Britain and, when returning home, into your own country:

| Into: | Cigarettes | Cigars | Tobacco | Spirits | Wine |
|---|---|---|---|---|---|
| Britain* | 400 or | 100 or | 500 g. | 1 l. and | 2 l. |
| Australia | 200 or | 250 g. or | 250 g. | 1 l. or | 1 l. |
| Canada | 200 and | 50 and | 900 g. | 1.1 l. or | 1.1 l. |
| Eire | 200 or | 50 or | 250 g. | 1 l. and | 2 l. |
| N. Zealand | 200 or | 50 or | ½ lb. | 1 qt. and | 1 qt. |
| S. Africa | 400 and | 50 and | 250 g. | 1 l. and | 1 l. |
| U.S.A. | 200 and | 100 and | ** | 1 l. or | 1 l. |

\* For non-European residents. (Eire: 200 cigarettes, 50 cigars, 250 g. tobacco.)
\*\* a reasonable quantity.

**Currency restrictions:** There's no limit on how much foreign currency you may import into Britain, and the export of pounds is no longer restricted. Check to see whether your own country has any regulations on import and export of currency.

**D** **DRIVING IN BRITAIN.** If you are bringing in your own car or one rented in Europe you'll need the registration papers and insurance coverage. The usual formula is the Green Card, an extension to the normal insurance making it valid in other countries. Virtually all driving licences are recognized in Britain.

The driver and front-seat passenger must use seat belts. If you're riding a motorcycle, you're obliged to put on a crash helmet, even if **110** you're only a passenger. Throughout the U.K., a driving licence is required even for mopeds (motorbikes) under 55cc. Sixteen is the lower age limit for riding mopeds, 17 for motorcycles and scooters.

**Driving conditions:** Need we repeat it? Keep to the left! If you're not used to this traditional mode of driving, pay special attention at corners and traffic circles (called "roundabouts")—the places most likely to confuse. After a few days, driving on the left will come naturally, though you'll always have to be on guard against your right-aiming instincts in emergencies.

Yielding: at roundabouts, traffic already in the circular pattern has precedence over cars entering; elsewhere, unless otherwise indicated, the most polite driver yields the right of way (often with a flourish of the hand). On zebra crossings (marked by flashing amber beacons and preceded by zigzag white lines) pedestrians have priority. By the standards of most countries, British drivers are amazingly courteous.

You may well be confused as you try to drive through London; direction signs are sometimes limited to information on route numbers or local districts halfway to your destination. Prepare your itinerary in advance; it will be easier if you have a passenger to act as navigator.

Unless you have strong reasons for driving in central London, it's far wiser to take public transport.

**Speed limits:** In built-up areas, 30 or 40 mph; on motorways (expressways) 70 mph; on other roads, generally 60 mph.

**Parking:** Overtime parking at meters in central London is punished by roving traffic wardens, who issue hefty fines. The amount of time you can stay at a meter, and how much it costs per minute or hour, is printed on the machine. For longer stays, or in the absence of an available space, use a multistorey car-park or outdoor parking lot. In certain zones beware of those invitingly empty meterless spaces marked "permit holders only". These are reserved for local residents who pay in advance for the privilege. If you invade their turf you may be towed away.

A yellow line along the curb means "no parking". A double yellow line means "no waiting". At night and on Sunday you can park along the single yellow line.

**Fuel and oil:** Gasoline is sold nowadays by the litre in most petrol stations, but Imperial gallons (about 10% more voluminous than the U.S. gallon) can still be met with occasionally.

Self-service stations usually have the lowest prices. Here, you generally pay at the cashier's, though coin-operated pumps are occasionally to be found. Apart from the central area, service stations are abundant everywhere. Attendants expect a few pence tip for any extra services rendered.

**D** **Traffic police:** Though helpful and tolerant towards foreigners, traffic police will show little sympathy in the case of blatant speeding and drinking offences (see below). Their vehicles may be anything from a Mini upwards, and often, but not always, marked with a POLICE sign.

**Drinking and driving:** If you plan to drink more than a sip of whisky or half a pint of beer you'd better leave the car behind. Penalties are severe, involving loss of licence, heavy fines and even prison sentences; and the law is strictly applied.

**Repairs:** Members of motoring associations affiliated with the British Automobile Association (AA) or the Royal Automobile Club (RAC) can take advantage of speedy, efficient assistance in case of a breakdown. London has garages specializing in most makes of cars, so spares should be no problem.

AA: Fanum House, 5, New Coventry Street, London S.W.1; tel. 954-7373

RAC: 83, Pall Mall, London SW1X 5HW; tel. 839-7050

**Road signs:** Britain has adopted the same basic system of pictographs in use throughout Europe. *The Highway Code,* an official booklet available at most bookshops, contains a comprehensive explanation of road usage and signs. Some written signs may not be instantly comprehensible:

| *British* | *American* |
|---|---|
| **Carriageway** | Roadway; traffic lane |
| **Clearway** | No parking along highway |
| **Deviation** | Detour |
| **Dual carriageway** | Divided highway |
| **Give way** | Yield |
| **Level crossing** | Railroad crossing |
| **Moped** | Motorbike |
| **Motorway** | Expressway |
| **No overtaking** | No passing |
| **Roadworks** | Men working |
| **Roundabout** | Traffic circle |

**E** **ELECTRIC CURRENT.** Mains supply is universally 240 volts A.C., 50 cycles. Certain appliances may need a converter. At the very least you'll need an adaptor (try the electricity department of one of the big stores in Oxford Street) for British sockets, which come in a variety of sizes.

**EMERGENCIES.** See also individual entries such as CONSULATES, MEDICAL CARE, POLICE, etc. For police, fire brigade or ambulance, dial 999 from any telephone (no coin required). Tell the emergency operator which service you need.

**GUIDES and ESCORTS\*.** Organized guided tours are scheduled at the top tourist spots such as Westminster Abbey, the Tower or the British Museum. Many varieties of city sightseeing tours are accompanied by professional guides.

For a personally conducted tour of the city or some of the sights, contact the London Tourist Board (see TOURIST INFORMATION OFFICES) or London Taxi Guides, tel. 584-3118.

If you would like company for a night out "on the town", try an escort agency (see "Escorts and Guides" in the yellow pages). For a fixed fee your escort—perhaps an unemployed actor or actress—will show you the town, take you round the stores, dine and spend the evening with you.

**HAIRDRESSERS\*.** The trend is towards unisex salons featuring elegant cut-and-blow confections. But traditional barber shops and more conservative ladies' hairdressers are still to be found in London. The premises are less lavish, and so are the prices (to which a 10% tip should be added).

**HOURS**

**Barbican Centre:** Tuesday to Saturday 12 noon–9 p.m., until 6 p.m. on Sundays, closed on Mondays.

**British Museum:** 10 a.m.–5 p.m. on weekdays, 2.30–6 p.m. on Sundays.

**Changing of the Guard:** *Buckingham Palace* daily 11.30 a.m. in summer, alternate days in winter; *Whitehall* 11 a.m. on weekdays, 10 a.m. on Sundays; *Windsor Castle* daily 10.30 a.m.

**Commonwealth Institute:** Monday to Saturday 10 a.m.–4.30 p.m., 2–5 p.m. on Sundays.

**Courtauld Institute Galleries:** 10 a.m.–5 p.m. on weekdays, 2–5 p.m. on Sundays.

**Imperial Collection:** 10 a.m.–7 p.m. daily.

**H**  **Imperial War Museum:** Monday to Saturday 10 a.m.–5.50 p.m., 2–5.50 p.m. on Sundays.

**Kensington Palace:** 9 a.m.–3 p.m. on weekdays, 1–3 p.m. on Sundays.

**London Dungeon:** 10 a.m.–4.30 p.m. daily (till 5.45 p.m. in summer).

**London Toy and Model Museum:** Monday to Friday 10 a.m.–6 p.m., till 5 p.m. on Saturdays, 2–6 p.m. on Sundays (usually closed on public holidays).

**London Transport Museum:** 10 a.m.–6 p.m. daily.

**Madame Tussaud's:** 10 a.m.–6 p.m. daily (until 5.30 p.m. in winter).

**Monument:** Monday to Saturday 9 a.m.–6 p.m. (till 4 p.m. in winter), in summer 2–6 p.m. on Sundays.

**Museum of London:** 10 a.m.–6 p.m. on weekdays, 2–6 p.m. on Sundays; closed on Mondays.

**Museum of Mankind:** 10 a.m.–5 p.m. on weekdays, 2.30–6 p.m. on Sundays.

**National Army Museum:** 10 a.m.–5.30 p.m. weekdays, 2–5.30 on Sundays.

**National Gallery:** 10 a.m.–6 p.m. weekdays, 2–6 p.m. on Sundays.

**National Portrait Gallery:** Monday to Friday 10 a.m.–5 p.m., 10 a.m.–6 p.m. on Saturdays, 2–6 p.m. on Sundays.

**Natural History Museum:** 10 a.m.–6 p.m. on weekdays, 2.30–6 p.m. on Sundays.

**Planetarium:** 11 a.m.–4.30 p.m. daily.

**Queen's Gallery:** daily except Monday 11 a.m.–5 p.m., 1–5 p.m. on Sundays.

**St. Paul's Cathedral:** Monday to Friday 10 a.m.–3.15 p.m. (4.15 p.m. in summer), Saturday 11 a.m.–3.15 p.m.

**Science Museum and Geological Museum:** 10 a.m.–6 p.m. on weekdays, 2.30–6 p.m. on Sundays.

**Sir John Soane's Museum:** 10 a.m.–5 p.m., except Sunday and Monday; closed on Bank Holidays.

**Stock Exchange:** 10 a.m.–3.15 p.m.

**Tate Gallery:** 10 a.m.–6 p.m. weekdays, 2–6 p.m. on Sundays.

**Tower Bridge:** 10 a.m.–6.30 p.m. daily (till 4.45 p.m. in winter).

**Victoria and Albert Museum:** Monday to Thursday and Saturday 10 a.m.–5.50 p.m., 2.30–5.50 p.m. on Sundays; closed on Fridays.

**Wallace Collection:** 10 a.m.–5 p.m. on weekdays, 2–5 p.m. on Sundays.

**Westminster Abbey:** 8.30 or 9 a.m.–6 p.m. daily (except during services). Westminster Abbey Treasures: 10.30 a.m.–4.30 p.m. daily.

**LANGUAGE.** You may not catch the quick, slick cockney of a London cabbie, but neither does the average Yorkshireman. Quite apart from problems of accent, even beautifully enunciated words may mean something quite different from what you'd expect. Transatlantic differences, for instance, are so numerous that full-scale bilingual (British–American) dictionaries have been published.

A sampler of the more flagrant differences (see also under DRIVING IN BRITAIN):

| British | American | British | American |
|---------|----------|---------|----------|
| bill | check (restaurant) | pavement | sidewalk |
| biscuits | cookies | perambulator or pram | baby carriage |
| bonnet | hood (of car) | petrol | gasoline |
| boot | trunk (of car) | public school | private school |
| caravan | trailer | to queue | to stand in line |
| chemist | druggist | | |
| first floor | second floor | (hotel) reception | front desk |
| ground floor | first floor | return | round-trip (ticket) |
| lay-by | roadside parking spot | single | one-way (ticket) |
| lift | elevator | surgery | doctor or dentist's office |
| lorry | truck | | |
| off-licence | liquor store | tube or underground | subway |
| pants | shorts (underwear) | | |

**LOST and FOUND PROPERTY.** Finding a lost object depends on where you lost it. If it was in a bus or on the underground, go to the London Transport Lost Property Office at:

200, Baker Street, London NW1 5RW (no telephone inquiries)

In a train, contact the railway terminal at which you arrived in London; in a taxi, the Public Carriage Office:

15, Penton Street, London N1 9PU (tel. 278-1744)

International Travellers' Aid helps arriving foreign visitors who've lost their money, passport, luggage, etc., and will also try to settle other

**L** problems. The office (open every afternoon and evening except on Christmas Day) is located at:

Victoria Station, platform 10 (tel. 834-3925)

Report any major matter to the nearest police station; unless you do, and demand a certificate while you're at it, your insurance company at home may not pay up.

**M** **MAPS.** News-stands, bookstores, service stations and automobile associations offer a wide range of maps. The best known and most comprehensive map of greater London with a street index is a book called the *Geographers' A to Z Atlas of London*. Every taxi driver carries one.

London Transport produces informative maps and charts of bus and underground routes, mostly free. They are distributed at the main underground stations.

Excellent road maps drawn to various scales cover the entire country in sections. The most detailed are government-sponsored Ordnance Survey maps, available in most bookstores.

The maps in this book are based on material by Johnston & Bacon of Edinburgh who also publish a large-scale map of London.

**MEDICAL CARE.** Britain enjoys fairly high standards of public hygiene, medicine and welfare, which should give you a virtually worry-free holiday. Restaurants are regularly inspected and maintain clean kitchens. You can drink the tap water with confidence anywhere.

Although the National Health Service obviously takes care of anyone in need of urgent attention, foreigners from countries outside the EEC have to pay for non-emergency treatment. Medical insurance is therefore strongly recommended. Your travel agent or regular insurance company will have modestly priced policies available. If you're taken ill, you must first see a general practitioner, whose task it is to diagnose, treat, and if necessary, direct you to a specialist or a hospital.

In case of emergency (but emergency *only*), dial 999 for an ambulance, the police or the fire brigade.

If you become ill outside normal consulting hours, but your situation doesn't warrant an emergency call, contact:

Middlesex Hospital, Mortimer Street, London W.1; tel. 636-8333

Royal Dental Hospital, 32, Leicester Square, London W.C.2; tel. 930-8831

Moorfields Eye Hospital, City Road, London E.C.1; tel. 251-0017

**Chemists.** The sign may often read pharmacy (never "drugstore"), but these establishments are usually referred to as chemists' shops.

The only all-night chemist in London is Bliss:

54, Willesden Lane, N.W.6; tel. 624-8000

**MEETING PEOPLE.** The reserved, controlled façade of the average Briton generally conceals an easy-going, good-hearted nature.

People want to be helpful but their traditional reserve often prevents them from taking the first step. Don't hesitate to ask for direction; it often breaks the ice.

You may be addressed as Sir or Madam by a waiter or clerk in a store or even a policeman. But you must never return the compliment; it might even be construed as sarcasm. Find out a person's name and use the formal address—"Mr. Smith" or "Mrs. Jones". No first names unless specifically requested. And if you don't know a person's name, start the conversation with "Excuse me".

Among young people, attitudes are much more relaxed. Making friends—in pubs or stores or even on the street—is no problem; you'll be on first-name terms straight away.

## MONEY MATTERS

**Currency.** Decimal currency was inaugurated in Britain in 1971. You'll catch on to the new system much more easily than the British did themselves, who for years after the reform continued mentally converting back into the "real" money of pounds, shillings and pence.

The monetary unit, the pound sterling (symbolized £), is divided into 100 pence, often called "p".

*Banknotes:* £1, £5, £10, £20, £50

*Coins:* ½p, 1p, 2p, 5p, 10p, 20p, 50p; £1

Two coins from the pre-decimal era are still in use: the 2-shilling piece (worth 10p and the same size as the new coin) and the 1-shilling piece (now worth 5p and the same size as the new coin).

For currency restrictions, see CUSTOMS AND ENTRY REGULATIONS.

**Banks and Currency-Exchange Offices.** The leading banks have branches in shopping streets throughout London, even in the suburbs. Virtually any neighbourhood bank will change your foreign currency or traveller's cheques. So will private currency-exchange offices which are found in many central areas. They're indicated, rather exotically, by a sign in French— *bureau de change*.

Banks are normally open for business between 9.30 a.m. and 3.30 p.m. **117**

**M** without a break, Monday to Friday, and some work on Saturday mornings. Branches at air and rail terminals and currency-exchange offices everywhere have longer hours and work on weekends as well.

If you want to buy more than just a few pounds you'll do well to shop around. Exchange rates may vary considerably; banks normally give a better rate than exchange offices.

**Credit Cards and Traveller's Cheques.** Credit cards are widely used. Hotels, shops and restaurants display symbols of the cards they accept on their doors or windows. Even the police take credit cards to bail out cars impounded for illegal parking.

Traveller's cheques, on the other hand, may be refused in some stores and restaurants, mostly due to unfamiliarity with foreign exchange procedures. It's best to change them in a bank or currency-exchange office. Take your passport as proof of identity when cashing traveller's cheques.

On the whole, it's not a good idea to offer foreign currency as payment. Except in a handful of large stores, the exchange rate you receive will be noticeably to your disadvantage and many establishments will refuse all but British money.

**Value Added Tax.** With Britain a member of the Common Market, practically all merchandise and services are subject to a sort of sales tax (VAT) which is currently 15%. Foreign visitors may escape this tax on certain conditions, but note that the scheme is operated only by certain large stores, small quality stores and specialist shops and, except in the case of large purchases, is hardly worth the trouble. Here's how to proceed: 1) have your purchases shipped directly to your home address; or 2) ask the store to forward them to your port of embarkation (not applicable if you're leaving by air); or 3) take the goods with you along with a detailed invoice from the store for presentation to the customs officer upon leaving the country; the tax will be refunded to you in due course.

**N** **NEWSPAPERS and MAGAZINES.** Britain's national dailies, from the sober *Times* to the racy *Sun*, are sold everywhere in the morning. Most news-stands also carry copies of the *International Herald Tribune*, edited in Paris, but printed in Britain. American magazines are also widely available.

While newspapers from Europe and the Middle East are easily obtained, periodicals from further afield in the English-speaking world are rare. If you're hungry for news of home, try your high commission or **118** national airline office.

Events in London are publicized in the afternoon papers and weekly magazines such as *What's On in London*. A magazine called *Time Out* lists conventional happenings plus many off-beat activities of "alternative London".

**PHOTOGRAPHY.** All those green parks and red buses make fine colour shots—if you're lucky enough to have some sunshine.

All leading makes and sizes of film are sold at chemists (drugstores), as well as department stores and souvenir shops. The easiest way to have your film processed is to drop it off at a chemists. Since developing and printing is generally not done on the premises, allow at least a week for the processing (two weeks for slides).

**POLICE.** It's basically true what you heard about those London bobbies: the *are* unarmed, they *are* helpful, and they *are* popular with the British themselves. But they're also inflexible law-enforcers, so don't count on leniency.

Country and town police wear essentially the same uniform with minor variations. Policemen in patrol cars wear peaked caps insted of the traditional helmets.

In case of emergency, telephone 999.

Oh, yes, don't call a policeman a "bobby" to his face: call him "constable".

**PUBLIC HOLIDAYS.** There are eight public holidays throughout the year. These are: New Year's Day, Good Friday, Easter Monday, May Day (first Monday in May), Spring Bank Holiday (last Monday in May), August Bank Holiday (last Monday in August), December 25 (Christmas Day) and December 26 (Boxing Day).

If one of these holidays falls on a Saturday or Sunday, the usual practice is to take it on the following Monday.

**RADIO and TV.** Two BBC channels and two commercial, independent TV networks broadcast from early morning till about midnight.

On radio, five BBC stations provide news, music and feature shows for all tastes, from rock (BBC 1) to classics (BBC 3). Several commercial radio stations strongly challenge the corporation's ratings. The BBC World Service (648 KHz/463 m.) provides excellent international news coverage. If you're yearning to hear a voice from home, you can pick up the Voice of America, Radio Canada International and other shortwave transmissions.

Daily newspapers carry full radio and TV listings.

**R**  **RELIGIOUS SERVICES.** The Church of England is the official church in England, but freedom of all religions is guaranteed. Virtually every major religious grouping in the world—not only among the Christian denominations but Jewish, Muslim and Buddhist as well—has a place of worship in London. Many hotels display listings of nearby churches and times of services, and the Saturday editions of the more serious newspapers usually give information on the most prominent services; the weeklies *What's On in London* and *Time Out* list some.

**T**  **TIME DIFFERENCES.** In winter, Great Britain is on Greenwich Mean Time. In summer (between April and October) clocks are put forward one hour.

| Summer time differences | | | | |
|---|---|---|---|---|
| New York | **London** | Jo'burg | Sydney | Auckland |
| 7 a.m. | **noon** | 1 p.m. | 9 p.m. | 11 p.m. |

Dial 123 for a time check.

**TIPPING.** Hotels and restaurants may add a service charge to your bill, in which case tipping is not really necessary. Otherwise, menus or bills specify "Service not included". You needn't tip in bed and breakfast houses. Likewise, cinema and theatre ushers do not expect tips. Likewise, barmen and barmaids in pubs are never tipped, though you may offer to buy them a drink in return for good service or a pleasant chat. See the chart below for further guidelines.

| | |
|---|---|
| Hairdresser | 15%, 4–5% to assistant |
| Hotel maid, per week | £3–4 (optional) |
| Porter, per bag | 20–25p |
| Taxi driver | 10–15% (10p minimum) |
| Tourist guide | 10% (optional) |
| Waiter | 10–15% (if service not included) |

**TOILETS.** In railway stations, parks and museums, look for a sign saying "Public Conveniences" or "WC" (for "water closet"). If you're asking directions, simply ask for the toilets or the lavatory (pronounced *lav*-a-tree). The British say just that: euphemisms will get you nowhere. In Britain a bathroom is a room with a bathtub in it; a restroom means nothing at all; and if you should ask to "wash up", your hostess will refuse to permit it. "Washing up" in Britain means washing the dishes.

**TOURIST INFORMATION OFFICES.** The British Tourist Authority has offices in various countries for your information before leaving home:

**Australia:** 171, Clarence St., Sydney NSW 2000; tel. 29-8627

**Canada:** 151, Bloor St. West, Suite 460, Toronto, Ont. M5SIT3; tel. (416) 925-6326

**New Zealand:** Box 3655, 97, Taranaki St., Wellington; tel. 553-223

**South Africa:** Union Castle Building, 36, Loveday St., P.O. Box 6256, 2000 Johannesburg; tel. 838-1881

**U.S.A.:** Suite 2450, John Hancock Center, 875 N. Michigan Ave., Chicago, IL 60611; tel. (312) 787-0490
612 S. Flower St., Los Angeles, CA 90017; tel. (213) 623-8196
680 5th Ave., New York, NY 10019; tel. (212) 581-4700

The London Tourist Board is concerned with tourist activities in and around London, but also provides tourist information on the rest of Britain. The head office to which mail inquiries should be directed is at:

26, Grosvenor Gardens, London SW1W ODU

The National Tourist Information Centre in the forecourt of Victoria Station, operated by the London Tourist Board, provides information on London and England, hotel bookings in London and selected centres throughout England, theatre and tour bookings, sales of tourist tickets, maps, etc. It is open from 9 a.m. to 8.30 p.m., seven days a week (8.30 a.m. to 10 p.m. in July and August).

LTB also operates an information centre in the Heathrow underground station, where hotel bookings can be made.

LTB tourist information centres are also located at Selfridges and Harrods department stores (open store hours) and, from April to October, in the Tower of London, West Gate (open same hours as Tower).

**T**

The London Tourist Board telephone information service operates from 9 a.m. to 5.30 p.m., Monday to Friday, on (01) 730-3488. At other times, call "Teletourist" (see COMMUNICATIONS).

For details on special events taking place within the City of London, consult the tourist information centre at St. Paul's Churchyard, London EC4; tel. 606-3030.

## TRANSPORT

**Buses:** Service is, technically, frequent on an extremely dense and complicated network of red double-deck buses. Free route maps and timetables are available at principal underground stations: Charing Cross, Euston, Heathrow Central, King's Cross, Oxford Circus, Piccadilly Circus, St. James's Park, Victoria and Waterloo (in the British Rail Travel Centre's office).

Make sure you're on the correct side of the road for the destination you want. At "request" bus stops, you must flag down your bus. At all others, every bus must stop. Don't forget to line up politely as the Londoners do, even though the habit is losing ground rapidly in face of the pressures of the modern world. If your bus is a conventional double-decker you climb aboard from the rear and take a seat; the conductor will come around and sell you a ticket *en route*. Just tell him your destination: the fare depends on distance travelled.

Single-deck Green Line buses serve the outskirts and nearby country-side.

Most buses run from about 6 a.m. to 11 or 11.30 p.m. A skeleton night service covers the main routes.

The "London Explorer Passes", valid for unlimited travel on both the underground and all London Transport buses in central and inner London, are sold for periods of one, three, four or seven days (for rates, see p. 102).

Similar special passes may be purchased for use on the Green Line country routes.

London Transport also offers a special "Red Rover" ticket, a one day ticket for travel on all red buses. Further information is obtainable at the London Transport travel information centres at the underground stations listed above, as well as from the:

Main Enquiry Office at 55, Broadway, London S.W.1 (tel. 222-1234).

**Underground** * : Often simply called the tube, this rapid, convenient network of underground (or, mostly, overground) trains criss-crosses the inner city and extends to many suburbs. Maps in the stations and trains, like ours on page 128, show the various lines colour-coded for easy reference.

The price of a ticket varies with the distance to be travelled. Buy your ticket in the station entrance hall, either from a vending machine (if you can figure out the fare and have the exact change) or at the cashier's. On your way to the platform you'll probably have to insert your ticket—face up—into a turnstile device which keeps tabs on all travellers. Don't forget to pick up your ticket when a split-second later it pops up again from the machine. Keep it throughout your voyage; you'll have to hand it in when you get out at your destination.

Before you take the stairs, lift (elevator) or escalator down to the platforms be sure you know a) which line you should be on, b) which direction you should be heading and c) where you'll have to get off or change to another line. Beyond central London some lines divide to serve more of the suburbs. Shortly before a train pulls in, a luminous indicator announces which route it will be taking. It's all far easier than it sounds—provided you avoid the rush hours.

For details on the "London Explorer Pass", see under "Buses" above.

Trains run from 6 a.m. to around midnight. There is no all-night service on any line.

**Taxis***: Those stubby black taxis, so much a part of the London scene, are spacious inside. Substantial luggage goes beside the driver (at an extra fee). If you want to chat with the driver you have to lean far forward or sit on the jump seat, for a discreet sliding window protects the passengers' privacy. London taxis are technically remarkable for being capable of extremely tight U-turns.

But the most astonishing thing about them is the encyclopedic knowledge of the drivers. To be licensed they've had to memorize the location of every street in London and the easiest way to get from one location to another. To avoid misunderstandings, be sure to tell the driver the postal zone of your destination as well as the complete name of the street: you must always specify "street" or "place" or "road" or whatever, otherwise, no one could possibly distinguish between, say, Grosvenor Gardens N.W.2 and Grosvenor Gardens S.W.1, or the dozens of other Grosvenor variations all over London.

Generally, all you do is hail a cab on the street when its yellow "For Hire" sign is lit.

Consult the yellow pages of the telephone book for the West End and Central London to obtain radio taxis.

Minicabs, normally lacking any distinguishing signs, may be ordered by phone. They are useful for late-night or exceptionally long trips.  **123**

**T**  If you take a taxi to a destination outside London the fare becomes subject to negotiation and should be agreed on before you start.

A 15% tip is customary, 20% if help with luggage is given.

**Trains:** The principal mainline (as opposed to underground) stations are Euston, King's Cross, Liverpool Street, Paddington, St. Pancras, Victoria and Waterloo. The underground connects with all of them.

The British Rail Travel Centre is located at:

12, Lower Regent Street, London S.W.1 (for callers in person only)

When buying a ticket you'll be given a second-class one unless you specify "first". Expresses are usually punctual, other trains… less so.

Various reductions are available for certain types of outings and for youngsters, oldsters and large families. If you intend to travel around the country a lot, consider a *Britrail Pass*, a flat-rate, unlimited-use ticket. But you have to buy it at your travel agency *before* you arrive in Britain.

**W**  **WEIGHTS, MEASURES and SIZES.** The metric system (decimalization was adopted in 1971 for British currency) is slowly centimetring its way into every walk of life. The situation is confused and confusing: metric weight and measures are reasonably familiar to young people (they are taught in schools) but incomprehensible to most people over about 35. Cloth is sold by the metre and wine by the litre but you still buy beer in pints. Temperatures are officially quoted in centigrade, but understood in Fahrenheit. Even the famous gallon is disappearing, being replaced by the litre.

### Length

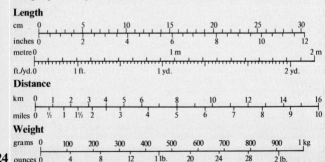

**Distance**

**Weight**

# Index

An asterisk (*) next to a page number indicates a map reference. For index to Practical Information, see p. 103.

127

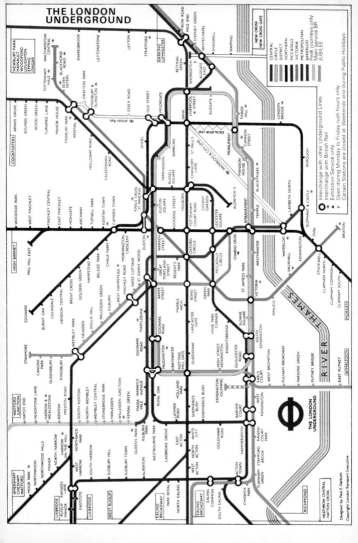

# THE LONDON UNDERGROUND

THE LONDON UNDERGROUND

Designed by Paul E Garbutt

Copyright London Transport Executive